FOREWORD

Reading Crying Wind's book was a delight for me. Having been in missionary work with the Navajo people for over 30 years, it brought back the many real-life situations that I have personally witnessed. I again saw the pathos, hopelessness, and utter lostness of the Indian, particularly the youth. The struggles in trying to go from one culture to another is graphically portrayed by the tremendous quality of Indian character and their tenacity to keep moving toward victory.

It has been my privilege to know Crying Wind, her husband, and family. I believe that this book is a valuable contribution toward better understanding of the American Indian by the Anglo culture. I gladly commend this book for your enjoyment and edification.

—Jack Drake
Founder and President
Navajo Missions, Incorporated

MY SEARCHING HEART

by

HARVEST HOUSE PUBLISHERS
IRVINE, CA

MY SEARCHING HEART

Copyright © 1980 by Crying Wind

Published by Harvest House Publishers
Irvine, California 92714

Library of Congress Catalog Number 80-83846
ISBN-0-89081-262-4

Printed in the United States of America.

This book was written with love for
my husband, Don,
and our children—
Little Antelope,
Lost Deer,
Snow Cloud,
Spring Storm—
who taught me the meaning of
love and laughter.

THE CROSS

On a hill there stood
Two strips of wood
To form a hated cross.

The ground was red
From the blood Jesus shed
On that hated cross.

That ugly cross,
That hated cross,
Where Jesus died for me.

That glorious cross!
That beautiful cross!
Where Jesus set me free!

CRYING WIND

5

Illustrations by
Crying Wind

Preface

"Whatever happened to Uncle Flint?" was the first question people asked when they met me after they read my first book, *Crying Wind.*

I was amazed at the overwhelming response to my book. When my phone started ringing and letters started pouring in from people who wanted to know more about the people in the book, I knew I would have to dust off my typewriter and finish my story.

In *Crying Wind* I told of the struggle of my family, who belonged to a different culture and believed in the old Indian gods, and what happened to us when we heard of Christianity for the first time. I tried to share the terror and loneliness of believing in a false religion.

Some of my experiences were left out of my earlier book because I felt they were too personal or too embarrassing to share. Now, since so many people have shown loving concern and interest in the details of my life, I have decided to share my deepest secrets in the hope they will be read with understanding and compassion. Being human, I've often said and done things that I wished later I hadn't. Because of this, I have changed some of the names and places to protect the privacy of those involved. It is not my wish to embarrass or criticize anyone. Time sequences were sometimes changed to make the story more interesting, but the details of the events were kept as accurate as my memory can recall.

7

If some of my experiences sound strange or impossible or just plain foolish, please remember that as a new Christian (with no church or Bible background), I matured very slowly and often found it hard to adjust to my new way of life. However, all the events in this book have actually happened to me or to those I love.

I'm very grateful to my good friends and patient husband who have helped me to grow and to find my place in the world, and especially to all those who read *Crying Wind* and cared enough to ask, "Whatever happened to Uncle Flint?"

Chapter One

Rifle shots rang out in the distance like thunder on a still night, and dust kicked up around my feet where the bullets hit the dry earth. I stood frozen in place. To move now, even one inch, could cost my life. Two more shots echoed down the valley, and again dust kicked up near my feet.

A nerve-shattering scream knifed through the air. "Today is a good day to die!" A young Indian man let out his war cry and whipped his horse into a breakneck run that ended in a sliding stop less than three feet from where I stood.

The Indian man wore only jeans and moccasins. His dark chest was bare to the hot sun, and his long, black hair fell loose to his shoulders. He had a gun stuck in his belt and held a rifle in his right hand. He threw his right leg over the horse's neck and slipped easily to the ground, allowing the horse to step off and search for grass.

My gun was cold and heavy in my hand as I slipped it from my holster and leveled it at the man walking toward me.

"Is it really a good day to die?" I asked.

He laughed as he stooped down to pick up an empty pop bottle and set it on his head.

I squeezed the trigger, and a bullet shattered the bottle into hundreds of tiny pieces. My Uncle Flint laughed and brushed the glass out of his thick, black hair.

"Good shooting, Crying Wind. Now it's my turn."

11

The gun was cold and heavy in my hand.

I picked up an empty tin can and held it in my hand. An instant later my uncle jerked his .44 Magnum revolver out of his belt and fired. The can flipped up into the air with a hole in the middle. He pulled the trigger again, and it had a second hole in it before it hit the ground.

"I wish it was hunting season," Flint said as he took a couple more shots at the can. "In the old days there were no hunting seasons. When you got hungry, you shot something and ate it. I'm bored with shooting at cans—and at you," he added with a grin.

"Are you going bear hunting this year?" I asked.

"Yeah, I saw lots of tracks less than a mile from the ranch. You want to come?"

I shook my head. There was nothing I feared more than a bear, and I was sure that someday I would be killed by one.

Flint threw a can into the air, and I grabbed his rifle and fired. He picked up the can and looked at the hole in it.

"You're one of the best shots I've ever seen, Crying Wind," he said.

I felt great pride rise in my heart. It was seldom my uncle had a compliment for me.

"You taught me how to shoot when I was five years old. You gave me my first gun when I was eight years old," I reminded him.

"Yeah, and the first thing you shot was Grandfather's truck!" He roared with laughter.

I wished he would forget that! Grandfather had beaten me for not doing my chores, and in anger I had shot his old truck full of holes. It had never run again. It had sat in the yard and rusted, a constant reminder of my black temper.

Eager to change the subject, I said, "I guess we've used about ten thousand bullets shooting together."

13

"Maybe. Never stop practicing, Cry. Someday your life will depend on how well you use your gun."

"In the old days, but not now," I said.

"Yes, now!" he snapped. "Times change, but people don't! People are dangerous. People are the same today as they were a hundred years ago, and they will be the same a hundred years from now. Mark my words, Cry, never let anyone take your gun away. Someday your life will depend on it. An Indian is no good without a gun." He reloaded his rifle. "There's too many laws around here! I can't breathe! I want to be free! I hear in Canada they treat Indians better than they do here. Do you think it's true?"

"I don't know. Couldn't treat them any worse, I guess."

"I want to go someplace, maybe back to the reservation, find something to do there. Maybe find freedom." He got a hopeful look in his eyes.

"What about your girl friend, Autumn Rose?" I asked.

Autumn Rose was a Pawnee girl Flint had met in the hospital after he had nearly been killed in a car wreck. She had nursed him back to health, and he'd fallen for her.

"I don't see her anymore. She's always wanting me to be a Christian and give up the old Indian gods. I won't stop being an Indian for her. She's Indian, she should understand!" he said bitterly.

I was silent. I had been a Christian only a few weeks, and I knew it was hard to give up the old gods and the old way of life. It was a heartbreaking struggle; and even though I had accepted Jesus as my Savior, sometimes the past sneaked up on me and I could still hear my old Indian god, the Wind, calling my name, and I wanted to answer. I still did not have my roots deeply planted in the Christian faith, and I often felt confused, frightened and lonely.

14

"I'll find an Indian girl who lets a man be what he is and doesn't try to change him. A good, obedient wife who will give me many sons, and she will grow old and fat and keep me warm in my old age." He nodded, agreeing with himself.

"And I will marry a strong, handsome Indian man with arms like two oak trees and long hair like a raven's wing. He will have hooded eyes like an eagle, and he will wear buckskin and beads!" I said, and my heart prayed that someday there would be such a man. A warrior, his name would be Winter Hawk or Running Wolf or Lightning Eyes.

"Flint, why is it we don't fit into this world?" I asked the question for the thousandth time. "What's wrong with us?"

"We're not wrong, we're just different. There's war drums in our blood, Cry; you and me, there's a dangerous fire always burning in our hearts. Sometimes only a tiny flame, but then it explodes into a wildfire, burning out all reason and caution and driving us to destruction. You and I are the kind who die for lost causes. We're driven. I see it in you when you are angry. Your eyes flash and you look like a wild animal. If you were cornered, you'd fight to the death before you'd give up."

"You're wrong."

"No, I'm not wrong. I know about you because I know about myself, and we are alike." He kicked a rock out of his way. "I feel fighting mad. I've been pushed enough! In the old days I'd have been a gunslinger," he said. He ripped his gun out of his belt and fired six shots so fast they sounded like one. "There's no glory or freedom in life anymore. Now there are only laws and rules. 'Don't do this, don't do that, don't be a man, don't think!' I can't breathe anymore!" Flint tossed a can to me.

"On your head!" he commanded.

The fear of appearing scared was greater than the fear of dying, and I obeyed. He shot the can off my head, and we both

15

holstered our guns. We were both deadly accurate shots, and we never missed; but if we had, it wouldn't have made much difference. Life was cheap to us; we had very little to live for. We were both lonely and drifting, and death was less frightening than life.

My seven uncles were my only family. My own parents had abandoned me when I was born, and Grandmother had taken care of me until she died shortly after my fifteenth birthday. Since then, I had been on my own, working here and there at countless jobs, earning just enough to survive.

Flint and I had had bitter feuds, and several times he had beaten me for attending a "white man's church" and turning my back on the old ways. After his near brush with death we had become close again, and we both avoided bringing up anything that would cause trouble between us.

After Grandmother had died, my seven uncles had scattered from the reservation. One uncle had committed suicide; one was in prison for robbing a bank. Uncle Kansas was always getting into trouble wherever he went, and two uncles had disappeared and we never heard from them again.

My favorite uncle, Cloud, had gone to Oregon, fallen in love, and become a Christian. He worked as a guide at a hunting and fishing lodge.

Everyone was far away now, and only Flint and I were left.

Flint and I mounted our horses and headed back to the ranch where he worked. We let the horses walk slowly along the worn trail, neither of us eager to end the day.

"Crying Wind," he said suddenly breaking the silence, "let's go home!"

"Home? We don't have a home." I shrugged.

"I mean the Kickapoo reservation! Let's go back to the reservation!"

"Do you mean it?" I was afraid he was teasing.

"Let's go tomorrow. I'll pick you up early. Pack all your stuff, you won't be back. We're going to be free!" He let out a war cry and jabbed his heels into his horse's sides, sending it into a wild gallop.

I let out a yell and whipped my horse into a run. We were going to be free!

My horse trailed far behind Flint, and I watched him up ahead of me, the sun glistening on his bare back, his muscles straining with the horse as they raced for freedom.

Freedom! Was it possible? Could we go back to the reservation and live the way we wanted to?

Excitement pounded in my chest, and I leaned down low on my horse and kicked it until it caught up with Flint. We raced side by side, yelling and laughing and filled with the hope of a free life.

That night in my apartment, I packed my few belongings into a cardboard box and prepared to leave. I didn't own much, and I was packed in fifteen minutes.

I started to call my boss to tell him I wouldn't be in the next day, but I decided not to bother. I was probably going to be fired soon anyway. I had already had eight jobs so far that year.

I pulled on my leather-fringed coat and walked to my church. I had to tell Reverend McPherson and Audrey good-bye. They were my best friends and had stood by me when I needed them. They had taught me about Jesus, and that had changed my life. It would not be easy to say good-bye to the only friends I had ever had.

They knew as soon as I stepped in the door that I had something on my mind, and I didn't waste time on small talk.

"I came to say good-bye," I said.

"Good-bye?" Audrey asked.

17

"Where are you going?" Reverend McPherson closed his Bible and folded his hands. He had heard me say good-bye many times since we had first met, and always after a few days or a few weeks I would be back again.

"Flint and I are going back to the reservation. We're going back for good. I won't see you again, but I'll write and let you know how I am." I was trying to take the sting out of the good-bye.

"What will you do there, dear?" Audrey asked, looking worried.

"Oh, I don't know. Maybe a little hunting, a little farming. We'll do all right."

"Do you really think this is the best thing for you? Your Uncle Flint, will he—" Her voice trailed off. She was remembering the terrible fights we had had in the past.

"Oh, he's OK. We don't fight anymore."

"But is there a church on the reservation? You must remain strong in the Christian faith. Don't go back to your wind god. You've only been a Christian a few weeks—you'll need Christian friends and a church."

"Don't worry, I'll take the Bible you gave me, and even if I don't get to church I'll read it."

Audrey's shoulders sagged. "Crying Wind, you must be careful. God has a plan for your life. You must not spoil His plan for you. You are so careless with your future; you never make plans."

"Yes I do," I argued, "I plan to go to the reservation."

"Then what?"

"Then we'll figure out what to do next," I said, hoping Audrey wouldn't give me her usual lecture about getting a good, steady job with a future. She couldn't understand why I couldn't hold a job more than two months or why I changed apartments every

18

four months. She didn't know what it was like to be restless and lonely. She was a good friend, but she didn't understand Indians.

"Crying Wind, do you really have to go? This is so sudden. Can't you think it over awhile? You have a pretty good job, and your apartment is nice," she argued.

"I don't like my job, and my rent is only paid until the end of the week."

"Oh, my dear child! When will you ever settle down?"

"Never, I guess. The wind calls me, and I answer. I need to be free. Don't you remember that even the name of my tribe, Kickapoo, means 'He who moves about'?"

"But you are a young girl! It's different for a girl. You can't just pack up and run off all the time."

"But I'll be with my Uncle Flint."

"But—oh, Crying Wind!" she sighed.

"We are going looking for freedom," I explained.

Reverend McPherson broke in, "Freedom is not something you go look for, it is something you feel in your heart. Who owns your heart, Crying Wind?"

"The wind owns my heart." I knew I should have said that God owned my heart, but old ways were hard to break.

"If you need anything, write to us or call collect, and we'll help you in any way we can. We are always your friends. You can come back here anytime you want to." Reverend McPherson shook my hand.

"We will miss you, Crying Wind, but if this makes you happy, then good luck and Godspeed," he said.

Audrey hugged me, and with tears in her eyes she said, "God bless you! Keep in touch with us."

"I'll write as soon as we're settled," I promised and hurried out into the night, anxious to get away from them before the

19

lump in my throat grew any larger. I missed them already. I owed them my life. When I had felt deserted and all alone, I had attempted suicide, and they had picked up the pieces. I had depended on them for so much. Now I wouldn't have their strength or friendship to lean on, and I wasn't sure how far I could fly on my own wings.

Chapter Two

I was already sitting on my box of clothes outside my door when Flint drove up at dawn. I threw the cardboard box into the back of the truck and climbed in beside him.

"Is that all your stuff?" He jerked a thumb toward my box.

"Yeah, I don't own much. Where's your stuff?"

"I own less than you do. I'm wearing most of it, and the rest is under the seat. How come we work so hard and don't have anything to show for it?"

"I don't know," I said, "I guess we spend it too fast. I never could figure out how people could save their money. I'm always broke."

"Well, don't worry about it. Back on the reservation we'll do better." He raced the engine and the truck roared down the road toward home.

Thirteen hours later we drove onto the reservation, tired, dusty and hungry.

As the pickup bounced and rattled down the muddy ruts in the narrow road our spirits sagged. The reservation was nearly deserted. Most of the shabby, two-room wooden houses stood empty. There was no livestock to be seen; tumbleweeds had taken over the pastures.

"Where did everybody go?" I whispered.

Flint drove down the back roads where our friends and family used to live, but no one was left.

21

Finally we spotted an old man plowing with a mule. Flint stopped the truck and walked across the freshly plowed field to talk to him.

I could see the old man shake his head no to everything Flint asked him, and in a few minutes Flint came back to the truck.

"Everybody's dead, moved away, or gone to the reservation in Oklahoma. The old man said there are only about fifty families left on the reservation now, and they are mostly old people like himself, who are too old to leave. He said just pick an empty house and move in." Flint didn't look as happy as he had earlier.

"What about the Banakee family?" I asked.

"All dead."

"But what about the Cadues?"

"Same. All dead."

"The Charlie Big Horse family?"

"Moved to the reservation in Oklahoma. I don't think we know anybody here anymore," Flint said.

"Flint, have you ever wondered about what happens to all the Indians after they leave the reservation?"

"They get lost in the crowds, I guess. They change their names, cut off their hair, buy a suit, and pretend to be something else besides Indians."

"Flint—" I swallowed hard. "I passed for white once," I confessed with shame. "I wore clothes like everyone else, dyed my hair a light color, and changed my name."

"What happened?" he asked.

"It was awful. I looked like a freak, I made some enemies, and I was miserable! The worst part was that after I came to my senses and saw how stupid I was and decided to be myself again, the people who knew me when I was passing for white wouldn't believe I was Indian! Even now people will say, 'I used to know you—you aren't Crying Wind, you are a white girl named Linda.

22

Why are you trying to be Indian?' It confused a lot of people. Some people said I was Indian, some said I was white. I guess since I'm a half-breed they were both right. It just goes to show you that you never really know everything about anyone. You only know what they want you to know, just the outside." I felt ashamed. "I wish I'd always just been myself and not tried to be somebody else."

"I know. My friend Black Hawk tells people he's a Mexican and calls himself José González. He says it's better to be a Mexican than an Indian."

"Is it better?" I asked.

"He's drinking himself to death. I guess that's the answer," he said grimly. "We'd better find a house before dark and move in." He turned down another narrow road and before long stopped in front of an old house.

We got out of the truck and walked inside the house. Pack rats scurried across the floor, and I quickly scurried back to the truck.

"I'm not staying here!" I said.

"It's getting dark. You sleep inside the truck, and I'll sleep in the back. Tomorrow we'll look for a good place to stay."

Flint climbed into the back of the truck and pulled his coat over his shoulders. I rolled up in my blanket and, trying not to get my feet tangled up in the steering wheel or bump my head on the door handle, lay down on the seat. Somehow this wasn't how I had pictured our homecoming. I was glad the McPhersons couldn't see me now, and I wished I had a nice, warm bed and something to eat.

I looked out the windshield and watched the stars come out one by one. Finally the moon decided to wake up and climb into the sky. There was a new moon that night: it was tipped so you could hang your powderhorn on it and keep it dry. The rain

23

would be held up in the sky all night. I was glad Flint wouldn't get wet as he slept in the open.

At last I began to grow sleepy, and I folded my hands and prayed, "God, this is Crying Wind talking. Did you see that I moved back to the reservation? Help Flint and me. Good night." I hadn't had much practice praying, and I didn't know God very well yet, so my prayers were short and without any fancy trimmings.

The next morning Flint sent me after a rabbit. It is easy to run down rabbits, because they run a little way and then stop, run and stop. They do this three times, and after they stop the fourth time they make a sharp turn to the right or left. You don't have to outrun them, you only have to outguess them. After a couple of misses I caught one by the nape of his neck and carried him back to Flint. We cooked him over an open fire. He was a skinny rabbit, but at least we had some breakfast.

We began driving down all the back roads, and just before noon we found a house that hadn't been empty long. We moved into it before the pack rats did. It had three small rooms, no furniture, no water, and no electricity. Flint drove into the trading post and bought some food and supplies, and by evening we were fairly comfortable and enjoying a hot supper.

The next day Flint got a job breaking horses on a nearby ranch, and I began planting a garden. We had a home; we were going to stay. Things were looking good for us. Now I could write to the McPhersons and tell them they didn't need to worry about me anymore.

A few days later I was planting some onions in my garden when Flint drove into the yard and stopped in a cloud of dust. He yelled out the truck window, "Cry, I know where you can pick up a fast twenty dollars."

"If it's such easy money, how come you don't pick it up yourself?" I laughed. Flint always knew a way to pick up easy money, but it never worked out. As often as not, he would end up working for nothing or losing money.

"Out on the ranch where I'm working there's a new colt the boss wants broken. I'm too heavy. He wants someone light on its back the first time."

"Oh, no thanks! I remember when you were riding in the rodeo a couple of years ago and entered me in the wild burro race! You said I was a cinch to win, but the burro I drew went everywhere except forward, and I came in last! I don't think I want any of your easy money!"

"This is different. It's just a nice little bay colt. You shouldn't have any trouble staying on him at all. You used to ride Thunderhooves like you were glued on her. I know you can handle this horse."

Memories of Thunderhooves flashed through my mind. It was a long time since she had died, and I hadn't ridden much since then. Flint took my silence as assent.

"No time like now. Let's go on out to the ranch and give it a try," he said and opened the truck door for me.

An hour later I was sitting on a corral fence looking at the little bay colt. Except he didn't look so little, and he was older than a colt.

"Flint, I don't think I want to do this. He looks mean," I said, backing down off the fence.

"He's as gentle as a lamb. Just let him know who's boss. Come on, Cry, you're acting like an old lady."

Flint patted the horse on the neck, and the horse tossed his head and shied.

"I don't feel good about it, Flint. The horse will know it, and I'll get thrown."

"Cry, it's just a little horse. Just get on and ride him around

25

Easy Money

the corral a couple of times so he can get the feel of somebody on his back. Then you can collect your twenty dollars, and we'll go back to town. Besides, I already told the boss you'd do it."

I walked slowly over to the horse and touched his back. He shivered and snorted. "What's his name?" I asked.

"What difference does it make? You don't have to be introduced to walk around the corral one time," he answered impatiently.

"What's his name, Flint?"

"Cyclone."

"What? You have to be crazy! I'm not getting on a horse named Cyclone!"

"It's only a name. We can call him Powderpuff if it will make you feel better. A dumb horse doesn't know what his name is."

I patted the horse and swung up onto his bare back and took the reins from Flint.

The horse shook and stepped sideways. Then his ears lay back and I dug in with my knees. Cyclone pitched forward and bucked three times, kicking his hind legs out behind him. Then he seemed to remember his name and spun around and exploded in all directions at once! He tucked his head so far back between his front legs that his neck disappeared, and I went flying over his shoulders, neck, and head. I hit the ground headfirst and started rolling head over heels across the corral until I hit one of the fence posts. I felt my neck pop, and I lay in a crumpled heap.

Flint grabbed the rope on the horse and tied him snugly to the gate. Then he gave the rope a final jerk and came running to me.

"Cry! Are you all right?" He kneeled down beside me.

I looked up at him, but everything was spinning around so

27

fast I closed my eyes to make it stop. "My neck! My neck's broken!" I yelled.

"Can you straighten it? Can you move your head?" Flint asked.

I tried to move my head, but it hurt so much I thought I was going to be sick. "It hurts too much. I can't move!" I could feel my head resting on my right shoulder, with the muscles pulled tight on the left side.

"Can you move your arms and legs?" Flint was starting to sound scared.

I moved my arms and legs a few inches.

"You're neck isn't broken if you can move—it's just bent. I'll pull it back into place." He reached over and put one hand on each side of my head and tried to straighten it.

Everything went white and I screamed with pain. "No! No! Don't touch me! Flint, my neck is broken!"

"No it's not, you just had a bad spill. You'll be all right." He picked me up and carried me to his truck, but when he tried to sit me up in the seat I started to get sick, so he carried me around and laid me down in the back of the truck. "I'll get you home and into bed. You'll be all right in a while."

As the truck bumped along the dirt road back to the old house, every inch of my body ached, and I could feel a large bump swelling up in the middle of my back. "I couldn't hurt this bad unless something was broken," I groaned.

After we got home Flint held hot, wet towels on my back while I held them on my neck, which was still bent at an angle.

"Flint, when I get well—if I ever do—I'm going to kill you!" I said through clenched teeth.

"It was just a bad spill. You'll be fine tomorrow. You can take it, Cry, you're tough." He took away the hot packs from my

28

back and looked at the swelling. "Cry, do you think you need a doctor?"

"Does it look that bad?" I was glad I couldn't see it.

"It doesn't look good." He put the hot pack back on. "Let's wait an hour. Then we'll decide."

We both looked at the clock fifty times during the next hour. My dizziness was gone now, and my stomach was reminding me that I hadn't eaten all day. Flint cooked some bacon and eggs for us, and I began to feel as if I might live.

I stayed in bed the next day. Each day my neck got a little straighter, and by the end of the week it was back in place again and I was no longer looking at a crooked world.

Flint got over being worried, and in two weeks he was thinking up more ways to get us some "easy" money.

The first Sunday I was on the reservation I dressed up, took my Bible, and walked a mile to the little wooden chapel.

There was no one around when I arrived, so I sat down under a shade tree to rest and wait for the others to come. I kept thinking I had come too early, but after a while I realized no one else was coming.

I walked down the hill for a closer look. The white paint had peeled and chipped. The tower held a silent bell, and just below the cross was a small, crooked sign, which read, "KICKA-POO BIBLE CHAPEL."

The doors were nailed shut, so I walked around to the side of the building and peeked through the dirty windows. Inside were rows of dusty pews, and the pulpit was lying on its side. The chapel was empty. It hadn't been used in years.

"Closed due to lack of interest," I whispered. What had happened to all the people who had built such a fine church? Where were they now? I knew many of the younger people were going

29

back to the old Indian religion, but surely, somewhere on the reservation, there must be a few Christians. Why had they closed up their church?

I felt sad as I looked at the empty chapel. It looked like an old woman sitting there. All her children had gone away and left her alone to die on the prairie.

DESERTED CHAPEL

Chapel on the plains,
Beaten by wind and snow and rains,
Sad and lonely standing there,
A silent monument to prayer.
Weddings, christenings, funerals, and praise
Marked the memories of your days;
Now dust blows through the broken door,
Weeds grow through cracks in the floor.
The pews are now empty, they once were filled;
The voices of praise have long been stilled.
The people are gone, the houses are too;
Time has taken all but a few.
The old wooden cross reaches up to the sky,
As a welcome to strangers who may pass by,
But no one comes here anymore,
No weary travelers will stop by your door.
Chapel on the plains,
Beaten by wind and snow and rains,
Sad and lonely standing there,
A silent monument to prayer.

Deserted Chapel

Chapter Three

We had been back on the reservation a few months but knew very few people, so I was surprised when there was a knock on the door late one evening. When I answered it there was a man holding a paper bag of fresh garden vegetables.

"Is your uncle home?" he asked, looking past me into the house.

"No, he's gone out tonight," I answered trying to remember if I had seen this man before.

"He asked me to bring these by, but since he's not here, I'll just leave them with you," he said and held the sack out in front of him.

I opened the screen door and reached for the sack, but he threw it aside, spilling the vegetables across the porch. He grabbed my wrists and shoved me into the house. Once we were inside he let go of my wrists and quickly looked around to make sure I was alone.

I was in trouble! I had made two mistakes: I had told him I was alone, and I had opened the door for him! How could I have been so stupid? I glanced around the room to see what I could use for a weapon. There was a poker by the stove, but I wasn't sure I could hit him hard enough to knock him out. What if I just hit him hard enough to make him angry, and he killed me?

I backed up a step. "So you are a friend of my uncle. Do you work with him?" I asked, trying to keep my voice from shaking. "What?" He turned around to face me, and then I could tell he was drunk.

"I asked if you met my uncle at the ranch. He'll be home soon now. He'll be glad you stopped by." I knew that if Flint had a date that night it would be hours before he came home, and I hoped it didn't show on my face.

In my heart I was praying, *God, help me! God, help me!*

He took a step toward me and my heart turned to ice.

"It's so hot in here. Why don't we go out on the porch for a minute and get a breath of that cool evening air?" I smiled at him and stepped out the door. He was right behind me as I walked to the edge of the porch.

It was dark outside now, but the light from inside the house shone through the window and lit up the porch.

"Oh, look!" I said, pointing off to his right. "Is that your dog?"

Without thinking, he turned to look, and I leaped off the porch and headed for the trees at a dead run.

Please, God! Don't let him catch me! I prayed as I ran for my life.

I could hear cursing far behind me as he staggered through the underbrush.

I made as much noise as I could as I ran through the trees. It was very dark, and he was drunk; if he would follow me far enough, he would probably get lost. Now I began to move as quietly as I could. I wanted to make a circle and get back to the house. He could get lucky and stumble across me, or maybe he wasn't as drunk as I thought. I couldn't underestimate him.

I silently worked my way back toward the house. Then I was

out of the trees and running across the open yard. If I could just get inside the house! I reached my bedroom window and climbed through it. I shut the window behind me and hurried to my closet. Even though it was pitch black, my hand reached inside and found the shotgun.

Now I waited. Would he try to get back into the house?

There! A noise on the porch! He was back! I watched the doorknob and waited for it to turn. Nothing happened. I could hear vegetables rolling across the porch. I knew he was out there!

I took a deep breath. "Get out of here or I'll shoot!" I yelled. I slid the bolt into place and held the shotgun waist high. "This is your last chance!"

I counted to three and fired at the door, splintering it.

A few seconds of silence, and then an engine started! I looked out in time to see a pickup truck pulling away.

I ran out onto the porch and fired the shotgun after it. *Blam!* One of the taillights went out. *Blam* again! But he was out of range. His wheels were spinning, and the air was thick with dust he was kicking up. I shot again. *Blam!* He was far down the road now. He must have been driving ninety miles an hour.

I went back into the house, locked the door, and reloaded the gun—just in case. I let out a shaky breath. "Thank you, God," was all I could say.

When Flint came home hours later I spilled out the story of the frightening nightmare.

"Well?" I said after I had finished. "What are you going to do?

I expected him to grab a gun and go after the man.

"You handled it all right," he said and pulled off his boots. "Guess I still think of you as a kid. I never thought about any

34

man giving you trouble. Better keep an eye on you from now on," he yawned.

I was disappointed. I felt that he should have been angry, but instead he was calmly getting ready for bed.

"If a man came and stole your rabbits, you would punch him in the nose! If a man tries to steal me, you don't do anything! I'm worth less than a rabbit to you!" I was angry.

He smiled. "Cry, you are safe. You probably scared that man so bad he drove down the road and had a heart attack. You probably scared him worse than he scared you."

"I doubt that!"

"I can't do anything tonight. Tomorrow I'll ask around and see if I can find out who he was. Then I'll decide what to do about it. Now forget it and get some sleep."

I went to bed, but it was a long time before I fell asleep.

The next night when Flint came home he was smiling the smile of someone who knows a secret. "I heard a couple of the men talking today," he said, grinning.

"What about?"

"About a man who needs some repair work done on his truck. It seems some wildcat shot his truck full of holes," he laughed. "I told them he was lucky the holes were in his truck and not in his hide! I said to pass the word that if he ever showed up here again, his hide would be nailed to our barn, and that went for anybody else who had any ideas about my niece." He threw his hat at the table and missed. "Nobody will bother you again."

The next morning my hammering caught Flint's attention, and he walked to the front gate to see what I was doing.

He stood behind me and read aloud the sign I was nailing up. " 'BEWARE OF BAD DOGS.' We don't have any dogs," he said.

"You don't have to have a dog to put up a sign," I said. I reached into a sack and took out three large soup bones and dropped them on the ground in front of the sign.

"That won't work," he laughed. "People aren't afraid of signs."

"Yes they are," I said and picked up my hammer and nails and headed toward the house. "It will keep bad people away." He fell into step beside me, still laughing and shaking his head.

Before we had reached the house we heard a horn honk and turned around. A large, red car had pulled up, and the driver was waving for us to come to him.

"What can we do for you?" Flint asked, walking toward the car.

"I'm Bright Star's cousin. She said you'd sell me some rabbits," the driver said.

"How many do you want?" Flint asked.

"Four."

"Come out back to the hutch, and I'll let you pick out the ones you want," Flint said.

"No thanks! I don't hanker to get chewed up by your dogs."

"Dogs?" Flint asked.

"I saw your sign. That's why I honked instead of getting out of the car. I'm too old to outrun a pack of bad dogs. I'll just wait here, and you bring me four rabbits." He handed Flint eight dollars.

Flint shoved the money inside his shirt pocket. "Well, I'll be!" he whispered as he walked past me. "It does work! People are afraid of signs!"

Flint stayed closer to home, just as he had promised, and the man never returned. But in spite of this, I never felt safe again. I watched for movements in the bushes, for shadows that didn't belong, and I listened for footsteps behind me. I went inside early and locked the house up tight before sundown. I checked the locks on the doors several times before I went to bed, and often I didn't sleep well. I began to realize that I was not safe by myself; a girl alone is in danger. My safety depended on Flint. If he left, what would I do?

Chapter Four

The garden was breaking up through the soil. The corn plants were young and only a few inches high when Flint announced it was time for the Green Corn Dance and powwow.

I jumped up and down with excitement on the day of the ceremony. As we drove to the campgrounds, we could see many trucks and crowds of Indians getting ready for the dances to begin. We pushed our way through the crowd to get a better place from which to watch the ceremonies.

Flint was wearing a new western shirt, and I was wearing my buckskin dress and had beads in my hair. Most of the Indians had on traditional tribal clothing to honor the day. The Green Corn Dance was performed to ask the corn to grow tall and give food to the people so they would not go hungry the next winter.

Indians of several tribes lined up facing east across the dance grounds. Silence fell over the crowd, and for several minutes we stood waiting.

Then, like a thunder of drums, fifty screaming Kickapoo warriors came charging over the crest of the hill on galloping horses.

My heart leaped with emotion and tears stung my eyes at the sight of the young braves on half-wild horses swooping down the hill in a cloud of dust. No wonder Kickapoo warriors had terrorized the early settlers! Even now they were a fearful and wonderful sight!

Their wild charge ended in a horse race. The winner would be given the horse of the man who finished last.

As the horses raced across the open plains my eyes looked upon one of the riders, and my heart rode with him. He was young, and his arms looked as strong as oak trees. His long, black hair flew in the wind, and around his neck was a necklace of old Indian trade beads. He was a wonderful rider and had a fast horse, but he didn't win the race. A boy on a gray horse won. But it didn't matter to me, because although my warrior had lost the race, he had won my heart.

All morning I tried to catch glimpses of him in the crowd, and it didn't take Flint long to figure out whom I was watching.

"Do you want to meet Yellow Thunder?" Flint asked, smiling. "I know an uncle who can arrange it."

"How do you know his name?" I repeated it to myself. *Yellow Thunder.* It rang like music in my ears.

He laughed. "He sells horses to the ranch where I work. Aren't you lucky to have me for an uncle!" Flint said and looked very satisfied with himself.

True to his word, Flint introduced me to Yellow Thunder, and my heart pounded so loudly I was sure he could hear it. He smiled at me, and when I looked into his eyes I knew I was in love for the first time. It had hit me suddenly and without warning. It was like being caught in a rock slide, and my life was changed forever.

Each day after that I waited for Yellow Thunder to call on me. I looked out the window hundreds of times, and each evening I combed my hair and sat in the yard and waited. Surely he would come tonight!

I had great dreams about our life together—secret dreams that I kept hidden in my heart. I was sure that if I loved Yellow Thunder enough he would have to care a little for me in return.

Yellow
Thunder

Wrapped up in thoughts of the handsome warrior, I grew more quiet each day. One day he would come. I would be patient, I would wait for him. Each day I watched, each night I waited. Weeks passed, and my feelings for him grew stronger.

Then one night he came! When he rode up the path and tied his horse to the fence I wondered if I was just dreaming again or if it could really be true!

I hurried out of the house to meet him, my eyes shining and my hands trembling.

"Hello, Singing Wind. Is Flint home?" he asked.

I was crushed. He had come to see my uncle, not me, and he hadn't even remembered my name!

He went inside the house, and he and Flint began talking about the price of a horse.

I sat down on the sagging wooden steps with my chin in my hand. *How could he not see the way I feel about him? He must be blind!*

I walked out and patted his horse for a few minutes and watched the sunset. Then I headed back to the house.

Their voices drifted through the open door, and I stopped when I heard Flint mention my name.

"Crying Wind looks your way, Yellow Thunder," Flint said.

My face burned in the darkness. Flint should not have told him that!

"Flint, you are my friend, so I will speak the truth to you. You and I are true bloods, but your niece is a half-breed. If she was a pure blood, things might be different, but I don't want any of my sons to be quarter-breeds. The girl I choose will have to be a pure-blood Kickapoo."

"She's a true-blood Indian in her heart, where it counts," Flint argued.

41

"It's our sacred trust to keep the bloodline pure and preserve our people," said Yellow Thunder.

As I stood there in the shadows of the night, the man I loved stabbed me in the heart and left me mortally wounded, like a rabbit with an arrow through its chest. Love had lost its sweetness and left me crushed and hurt.

Half-breed! That's all I would ever be!

I ran into the woods and wept bitterly. My first love had come and gone without even a touch of hands for a memory.

I heard the sound of hoofbeats fading into the distance.

"Good-bye, Yellow Thunder," I sobbed. "I'll never love anyone but you."

Flint came looking for me, and I dried my tears when I heard him approach.

"What are you doing out here?" he asked softly.

"Nothing," I choked.

He was silent. Far away lightning flashed across a purple sky and thunder growled.

"You heard, didn't you?" he asked.

I burst into tears.

"I wish I hadn't introduced you to him. Forget him, Crying Wind." He put his hand on my shoulder. "Let's go inside before it rains."

He led me through the darkness toward the house. He didn't speak again until we reached the front door.

A kerosene lantern burned brightly inside the house. I didn't want to step into the light and let Flint see my tear-streaked face, so I pulled away from him and sat down on the steps. "I'll come inside in a few minutes," I said between sobs.

He stood holding the door open and then said quietly, "It hurts, doesn't it?"

"Yeah, it hurts," I whispered.

He went inside, and just before he shut the door behind him he stopped and said, "Be tough, Cry. Always be tough. Then you never get hurt." He blew out the lantern and left me alone in my misery.

"I'll never love anyone again." I wiped away my tears. "Never! Never! Never! I'll be tough!" I vowed and went into the house.

After I had crawled into my bed, I lay awake for hours and listened to the storm come closer. I prayed the hurt in my heart would go away. I didn't know that when you are wounded by someone you love it never heals.

MY LOVE SONG

Alone in the dark night I dream of you,
When the sun is high I watch for you.
When I see you, the sky smiles, and my heart pounds
And I am afraid to look at you.
You pass me, and I do not raise my eyes,
But after you are gone I look up and watch the strong
    muscles of your back
Until you are gone from sight.
When it is sundown on War Pony Hills,
I long for you and walk in the night.
The wind carries your voice to me.
Oh, Yellow Thunder, hear my love song!
Together we will walk quietly on the rainbow trail.
I will give you sweet water of melted snow to drink,
You will hold your hand over my head to protect me.
On my fingers are rings of turquoise,
On my feet are moccasins with silver buttons.
Will you let me follow your path through the forest?

43

I wish you loved me as I love you.
My heart is filled with words my lips cannot say,
Inside I have songs I will never sing;
They are songs for you alone, and you do not hear.
When you leave, my heart grows dark and cold;
The sky weeps, and so do I.

Weeks passed, and a grayness settled over my days. Bugs and weeds took over my garden and killed our main food supply.

One night Flint finished supper and pushed his empty plate across the table. "Cry, it didn't work. There's no freedom here. The reservation is worse than the outside world. We're eating wormy vegetables and haven't had any meat in three days. I have one more horse to break, and then I'll be out of a job. We shouldn't have come here."

I didn't answer. If we hadn't come here, I wouldn't have met Yellow Thunder. If I hadn't met him, I wouldn't have to live with this dull ache in my heart. I closed my eyes and once again saw him charging over the crest of the hill with the rising sun behind him, his horse leaping and jumping. Yellow Thunder, with his black hair blowing in the wind and the war cry coming from his lips. Yellow Thunder—

"Crying Wind!"

Flint's voice brought me back to reality, and I began clearing off the table.

"I said this didn't work. We shouldn't have come back here." He paused. "I'm ready to leave. How about you?"

Leave? Never see Yellow Thunder again?

Flint poured the last of the coffee into his cup and cleared his throat.

"He's getting married, Cry. He chose a full blood, like he said he would."

44

I dropped the plates I was holding, and they crashed to the floor. My heart was in more pieces than the broken plates.

"I figure there's nothing here for us. Let's go back where we came from" he said.

"When?" I asked weakly and began picking up the broken glass.

"The sooner the better," he answered.

"Tonight?" I looked up.

He looked at me. "Why not? Get your box packed."

I forgot about the broken dishes and ran to my room. An hour later, all our belongings were in the back of the truck, and Flint started the engine.

Before going to the truck I took one last look around. The moon was coming up over the treetops, and I saw Yellow Thunder's face in it. "Good-bye," I whispered to him and shut the door to the old house. I knew I would never return to the reservation as long as I lived.

We rode in silence, each of us brooding over our broken dream. Flint had failed to find the freedom he was searching for, and I had failed to find love with Yellow Thunder. We drove all night, and early the next morning he left me on the McPhersons' doorstep with my box of clothes.

I rang the doorbell, and Audrey answered.

"You've come home!" she exclaimed and drew me inside the house.

"I don't have any money and no place to stay and no job," I said.

"You can stay here with us as long as you like," she said, just as I knew she would. She carried my box to the spare bedroom.

"You look very tired, dear. Would you like to lie down awhile?"

"We drove all night to get here," I said.

45

"What was your hurry?" she asked as she folded back the covers on the bed.

"We were running away," I answered and lay down.

"From what?"

"From a broken dream," I said and fell asleep before she pulled down the shade.

Chapter Five

Audrey and Reverend McPherson weren't the kind of people to say "I told you so," even when they had every right to say it. They didn't ask any questions, and I still hurt too much to tell them about Yellow Thunder. But I felt they somehow knew about him anyway.

I stayed with them a week, and then I found a job as a waitress in a coffee shop. They helped me find an apartment and lent me rent money until I got paid.

I was right back where I had started, except for one thing: now I knew how lonely I was, and night winds brought dreams of Yellow Thunder.

Flint was seeing Autumn Rose again, and he had started going to church with her. I was sure he would soon surrender his life to God and marry Autumn Rose. Things would work out for him now.

My own life was disappointing. I had thought things were somehow going to be perfect when I became a Christian. I had thought nothing would go wrong and that I would have a special power that would keep me from getting hurt or depressed or lonely. I had expected to have a magic shield around me that would protect me from the world. I had expected all my prayers would be answered YES and that I would be perfect and never make any mistakes. I had even hoped a millionaire would drive up in a white Cadillac and marry me and I would live happily ever after.

It didn't happen that way. The millionaire never showed up, I still made mistakes, and things still went wrong. God didn't answer all my prayers YES, and I was often depressed and lonely. Somehow it wasn't working out the way I had planned.

I began to have doubts about my decision. Maybe I was doing something wrong. Maybe I wasn't even really saved. Maybe I wasn't good enough to deserve God's blessings. Maybe God hadn't forgiven me for my sins. Sometimes the depression was so strong I felt as if I were buried in a black coffin. I felt guilty about being depressed. After all, Christians never got depressed, did they? And wasn't I really better off than most people? I was healthy, I had a few friends, I had my whole life ahead of me. I had many reasons to be happy. So why did I feel so miserable? My ups got higher and my downs got lower, and I was living on mountain peaks or in valleys, with no time in between. I remembered an old folk song that went something like, "From here on up, the hills don't get any higher, but the valleys get deeper and deeper." Was that true? Weren't there any higher hills to climb? Did the valleys get deeper and deeper?

My mind was traveling a dangerous path. I began to reason that life had little to offer and that death offered heaven, and wouldn't going to heaven be better than struggling along on this earth? After all, I was a Christian. I knew about heaven, and surely God wouldn't be angry if I came home before He called me. Once again thoughts of suicide crowded into my mind, but I was too ashamed to share my fears with anyone. It had been different before; I hadn't been a Christian. But now there was no excuse for my thinking, because I knew better. I began losing my grip on reality, and I spent hours daydreaming,

48

until the world in my mind was more important to me than the real world around me. I lived in daydreams, where I could make the world what I wanted it to be.

I attended church every time the doors were open, and I read my Bible and I prayed. But I felt separated from God, and there was a big, empty hole in my life.

I knew I was feeling sorry for myself and decided that if I could do something for others, I would forget about myself. I took a job at a nursing home and was sure I could find happiness and contentment serving others. I started with big plans and a heart full of hope. I went to work early and stayed late. But instead of feeling better, I felt worse, because the hopelessness of some of the patients began to find its way into my own life. I knew I wasn't helping them or myself, so after two weeks I quit.

I took a job in a candy store but was fired the second day because I was eating more candy than I was selling. I worked a week in a gift shop and was fired because I told a customer where she could buy the same dishes for half the price. In the next few months I changed jobs nearly every week and moved twice. I was looking for happiness in the wrong places. I thought happiness could be found in a place or a job or another person; I didn't know happiness depended entirely on my relationship with God. God had somehow slipped into second place in my life, and I was running in circles and wondering what I was doing wrong.

It was midnight, and there was a wild banging on my door. I got out of bed and pulled on my robe. It had to be one of my uncles—no one else in the world could make that much noise.

I swung open the door, and in staggered Flint and my Uncle Kansas.

49

Kansas was a year younger than Flint. His name was Kansas Kid, but we just called him Kansas. He was handsome and he was wild, and he felt no law ever made was meant for him.

"Kansas! I'm happy you've come!" I hugged him.

"Even in the middle of the night?" he laughed.

"Especially in the middle of the night!" It was true; I didn't sleep well anymore. When I crawled into my bed I found it was filled with memories that crowded out sleep.

"Where have you been for the last year?" I asked.

"Everywhere!" he laughed. "Wyoming, Montana, Arizona, Mexico. I've been driving trucks, training horses, trapping, and doing fifty different jobs in fifty different towns."

"What brings you back here?" I asked.

"I wanted to see what was left of my poor relations, and you and Flint are the poorest relations I know." He tugged at my hair. "How about some grub?"

"I can fry some bacon and eggs fast," I said and started to the kitchen.

"No! Eggs and buffalo steaks! Indians don't eat anything but buffalo!" He stomped his moccasined foot and shook his fist.

"I haven't had buffalo meat in years," I said, remembering what a treat it had been.

"What? Crying Wind no longer eats the meat of her ancestors?" Kansas demanded.

Flint joined in. "It's a disgrace! Let's go out and shoot a buffalo for Crying Wind!" And both Flint and Kansas disappeared outside.

They've been drinking, I thought to myself.

In an instant Flint came back inside and handed me three fresh steaks.

50

"What's this?" I asked.

"Buffalo," he answered.

"No, it's not," I argued.

That was what he was waiting for.

"Hey, Kansas, your niece doesn't believe this is buffalo meat! Prove it to her!"

Kansas came through the door holding the huge head of a freshly killed buffalo.

"A buffalo! It's a real buffalo! Where did you get it?" I exclaimed.

"Don't ask," Flint said. "Never ask where food comes from; just eat and be glad you have it."

Kansas set the buffalo head in my bathtub.

"Good medicine!" he said and patted one of the horns. He led me into the kitchen. "Indians need buffalo to live," he said. "If there were no more buffalo, there would be no more Indians. The Great Spirit gave us the buffalo. They belong to us. We have a right to kill them and eat them."

I fried the buffalo steaks and some eggs and made a pot of coffee.

"Kansas, even you cannot hunt buffalo in the city," I said.

"I found a piece of rope and put it in my truck. A buffalo was on the other end of the rope," he laughed.

"Where did you find the rope?"

"In the city zoo," he said and cut off a piece of meat.

"That's impossible! You can't steal a buffalo from the zoo!" I protested.

"A Kickapoo warrior can do anything he wants to do," he retorted.

I poured the coffee and silently prayed, *Forgive us, Lord, for eating this stolen buffalo.*

51

It was dawn when they decided to leave.

"Wait! You forgot to take the buffalo head with you!" I called after them.

"Don't be silly, Crying Wind. What would I do with a buffalo head? You keep it—it's good medicine," Kansas said.

"Kansas! I can't keep it in my apartment! It will start to smell!"

He stopped and came back inside. "You are getting fussy. How many girls do you know who have their own buffalo head?" he scolded.

"Kansas!" I pleaded.

"We need a safe place to keep it until it is dried out." He went after the buffalo head. "Pack some food, and let's go."

"I can't go with you. I have to be at work in an hour," I said.

"You won't spend one day with your uncle? After not seeing me in a whole year? And after I brought you this fine gift?" He held up the head.

"I'll lose my job! I've already had a dozen jobs this year," I explained.

"I've had fifty jobs this year. What difference does it make? You would rather go wait on tables than be out in the great, open spaces looking for a hiding place for Brother Buffalo?" he sighed. "You hurt your uncle's heart."

"OK, I'll go." I ran to the kitchen and started throwing food in a sack.

"Don't bring any meat," Kansas called after me. "We have five hundred pounds in the back of the truck. Just bring some bread, some ketchup, and some drinks.

As we sped down the highway we sang songs, laughed, and told lies to each other. Tomorrow I would be looking for a new job, but today was like old times. We would have fun, and we would be Indians again!

We drove a hundred miles away from the city, out to some sandy flats where the nearest ranch house was thirty miles away. There we found a small cave and hid Brother Buffalo's head and hide and pushed rocks over the cave opening.

Kansas threw the last rock into place. "Once we had thousands of buffalo here on this open range. Now we have to risk our lives to steal one back from the government," he said with bitterness.

The three of us felt a wave of sadness because we had missed out on our glorious past. We were three Indians who were born a hundred years too late, and there was nothing we could do about it. We didn't belong to the twentieth century any more than our friend Buffalo did. One day Indians would be extinct, too. Maybe the government would keep the last Indian in a zoo.

We ate a lunch of squaw bread and buffalo cooked over an open campfire.

Flint pulled a couple of guns out of the truck and he and Kansas did some target practice while I lay down on the warm sand and tried to catch some of the sleep I had missed the night before.

"Cry! Help me! I've been shot!" Kansas staggered over and, clutching his left shoulder, collapsed beside the campfire.

I sat up, blinking my sleepy eyes, and saw something red oozing between his fingers and dripping down his shirt.

"Quick! Do something!" He bent in half and groaned, "Flint shot me! I think I'm dying!"

I grabbed my jacket and held it against his shoulder.

"Flint! How could you! He's your brother!" I screamed at Flint, who stood nearby.

"Let me see where you are hit," I said to Kansas and gently wiped the blood from his shoulder. "I can't find the bullet hole."

53

I pulled open his shirt and found a perfectly healthy shoulder.

Kansas and Flint burst into hysterical laughter. "We sure fooled you! It was ketchup!" They slapped each other on the back and howled like coyotes. "Cry, you would fall for anything!" Can't you tell the difference between blood and ketchup?"

They were still laughing when we climbed into the truck and drove back to town. "I'll never believe a word you say again as long as I live!" I shook my fist at them. "That's what I get for caring about you wild animals! You've fooled me for the last time!"

Kansas moved in with Flint for a while. Luckily, I didn't get fired and still had a job when I returned from saying good-bye to Brother Buffalo.

A couple of weeks later I found Flint waiting for me outside my apartment. "Kansas has been shot," he said.

"Sure he has!" I snapped. "Don't you think you should stop wasting all that ketchup?"

"No, Cry, I mean it. It's no lie. He's really been shot, and he's hurt bad. I came to take you to the hospital to see him."

"Flint, if this is another one of your dumb jokes—"

"Not this time, Cry," he said in a tight voice, and I believed him.

It seemed like a long ride to the hospital, and Flint told me the story on the way. "He told the police it was an accident. He said that he was target practicing and tripped with his gun. He said he lost his gun. He said he drove back to town and tried to get someone to help him, but people thought he was drunk and just ignored him. It wasn't until he fell out of his truck and passed out that someone saw he was bleeding and called the police.

54

"Is he all right?" I felt sick.

"He was shot through the stomach. It's bad, but he'll make it." He paused. "He—never mind."

"What is it, Flint?"

"Well, I told you the story he wants people to believe. Don't ever repeat what I'm going to tell you now."

"I won't." I moved closer to him.

"Kansas was seeing some girl, and her family didn't like it. They already had some nice boy picked out for her to marry. Her brothers warned Kansas to stay away from her, but you know him. Well, one of her brothers shot him, and then he got scared and drove Kansas into town and dumped him out on the sidewalk. It's a wonder he didn't bleed to death before they got him to the hospital."

"Why didn't he tell the truth to the police so they could arrest the guy who shot him?"

"It's the girl he's protecting, not her brother. He doesn't want her mixed up in it. She doesn't even know it happened." Flint smiled. "Kansas said he was sure cured of any romantic feelings he had for her!" Then he warned me again, "Remember it was an accident!"

"I understand," I said.

Kansas developed peritonitis and was in critical condition. He drifted back and forth between life and death for days, and I was afraid gangrene would kill him the way it had killed my grandmother.

Flint and I visted him every day, and I constantly prayed for God to spare his life. Finally he began to improve, and I praised God for letting him live.

When Kansas was released from the hospital, he was supposed to stay in bed two more weeks, and the bandages on his wound needed to be changed every day. There was no one else

55

who could take care of him, so he moved in with me. He stayed in my bed, and I moved onto the couch.

He spent a lot of his time sleeping and reading paperback western novels. He really wasn't any trouble, except when it was time to change his bandage. I would swallow hard and hold my breath and try not to look at the big, bloody scab with the huge black and blue bruise around it. Each day changing the bandage got easier, and then it didn't bother me anymore.

One day he tossed his book to the foot of the bed and it slid to the floor.

"Got any more western books?" he asked.

"Don't you want to read something different? Aren't you tired of reading about people getting shot?" I asked.

He started to laugh but caught himself and put his hand over his wound. "You know, in the old days lots of cowboys got shot a half-dozen times during their lifetimes and then died of old age."

"You have five more times to go. Good luck." I laid some books on the bed—two westerns and two Christian books.

He picked up the two Christian books. "You can put these back."

"You should read them; they're good."

"I've told you ten times, I'm not interested in religion. I wish you'd quit preaching to me. I'm tired of hearing it!" he growled.

"I'll never get another chance to make you sit still and listen to me."

"Look, Crying Wind, I'll agree with you—I know the old way is dead. The Indian gods are false, but I don't believe in your God, either. I don't think there is any god of any kind, or this world wouldn't be such a rotten place. I don't believe in anything, because there's nothing to believe in. I'm going to have a good time while I'm here and then die, and that's the end of it."

I pointed to his wound. "You call that having a good time?"

He picked up a book and disappeared behind it. I didn't mention religion to him again, and a week later he left. I never saw him again.

Sometimes I would hear about his escapades from Flint. Kansas was arrested for trying to steal a bass drum from a band, and he was caught when, trying to make his getaway in a taxi, he got the drum stuck in the door of the cab. He was put in jail for three days for drunken mischief. He was arrested for trying to steal a buffalo from a private animal park, and he argued that Indians had the right to hunt buffalo as long as the sun shone and as long as the grass grew and that it was written in the treaties. He was fined fifty dollars and released. He was married several times and wrecked a dozen cars. He was racing to death and destruction as if his clothes were on fire, and nothing could stop him.

Then we heard Kansas was shot and killed in a barroom fight in Wyoming. When I heard the news I remembered how he had loved western novels and how he had said that some of the old cowboys had a half dozen gunshot wounds during their lifetimes. I wondered if he had really been killed because of a fight or if he had planned a suicide and had started the fight himself. If that were true, he couldn't have planned an ending that would have been any more like the plot of one of his western novels. "Killed in a gunfight in a saloon in Wyoming."

I missed Kansas. I missed his wildness and the reckless way he lived.

Years later I returned to the sandy plain where Flint and Kansas and I spent the day finding a hiding place for "Good

57

Good Medicine

Medicine," as we had named the buffalo. I found the cave and pulled the rocks away from the opening. I had expected to find a skull, but instead I found the buffalo head perfectly preserved. The hair wasn't even dusty, and the hide had turned to hard leather. I pulled it out by its horns and took a closer look. The skin had pulled back from the teeth as it had dried, leaving the buffalo looking as if he were smiling. Kansas would have liked that. Good Medicine, the Smiling Buffalo. I took the head home with me and kept it.

Sometimes my company would be startled to see a three-foot-high head of a buffalo in my living room, but I would just smile and remember Kansas and say, "How many people are lucky enough to own their own buffalo?" And I would pat one of the horns and add, "Especially one that smiles?"

Kansas, I miss you! Why were you in such a hurry to die?

Chapter Six

Flint and I sat at the table and let our coffee get cold. "Flint," I said, "our family is getting smaller. Grandmother died, Pascal killed himself, now Kansas is gone. Maybe you should get married and have some children, or soon there won't be anything left of our family."

"I think you're right," he said, and my mouth flew open in surprise.

"I've been thinking it over. I might as well take a wife. I'm tired of living alone. Autumn Rose is a hard worker and pretty. I guess she'll be the one."

"She's a Christian. She won't marry you if you aren't a Christian, too," I reminded him.

"I know. I've been thinking a lot about that, Cry. I think I might try out this new God you are always talking about. He helped you; maybe He'll help me."

It was all I could do to keep from shouting with joy.

"Flint, you'll never be sorry if you decide to believe in Jesus and be saved!"

"Might as well. What have I got to lose?" He shrugged.

He was acting as if he were treating the matter lightly, but I knew Flint never treated anything lightly. He had given it a lot of thought and had come to a decision. He looked embarrassed, and I knew he was waiting for me to say something.

"You'll be glad you chose Jesus. I'm proud of you, and I know you and Autumn Rose will be happy and have many sons. You can believe in God and still be an Indian. Being a Christian makes you more of a man, not less."

He looked relieved. "I guess I might as well get it over with, now that I've made up my mind. I'm going to see Autumn Rose tonight and set the date."

Now I was able to say something to Flint that I had been saving in my heart for months. "God bless you, my uncle!"

I was happy for him, but I was sad for myself, because I knew our old wandering days were over. Flint would have a wife and then children. He couldn't go running wild like the wind anymore.

Uncle Cloud came home for the wedding and stood with Flint as his best man. I looked at the two of them as they stood handsome and proud at the front of the church. The last of my seven uncles. Two were dead; one was in prison; and two were missing, and we didn't know if they were dead or alive.

I watched Flint and Autumn Rose as they pledged their love, and I felt a dull ache as I wished it could have been Yellow Thunder and myself being married that day. I closed my eyes and once again saw his face. When I looked up I saw the bride and groom coming down the aisle. I had never seen Flint so happy.

After the wedding Cloud drove me home. On the way, I said, "It made Flint happy to have you here today. He needed his brother beside him. I'm glad you came, too; I didn't think I'd ever see you again."

He smiled. "It's a miracle, Cry, the way you and Flint and I all believed in the old Indian religion and worshiped the old gods, and then within a few months we all heard the gospel for the first time and got saved. It's really a miracle."

61

I agreed with him and then asked, "Did you know Kansas stayed with me awhile? I tried to share our story with him, but he wouldn't listen. I felt terrible when he was killed." I took a deep breath and tried not to let my voice tremble as I asked, "Cloud, do you think—do you think Kansas went to hell?"

He chewed on his lower lip a minute before he answered. "I don't know, Cry. I don't think there is any way we can know who will be in heaven or hell until we die and get to heaven ourselves. The thief that died on the cross next to Jesus confessed and believed in the last minutes of his life, and Jesus said he would see him in heaven. Maybe Kansas did the same thing."

"I'd like to believe that," I said quietly.

"So would I," he agreed.

"Let's do believe it—maybe it really did happen that way," I said hopefully.

"Maybe," he said and changed the subject.

We began telling each other about all the things that had happened to us since he had gone to Oregon and left me in Colorado after Grandmother's death.

Then he spoke of his girl-friend. "I wish you could meet her," he said, and his eyes sparkled. "She is so sweet and gentle, like a fawn. She was the one who told me about God. We're getting married in the spring." He stole a quick glance at me to see my reaction.

"I'm happy you found someone. I hope you and Flint both have happy homes and many children."

"And what about you, Crying Wind? Have you found someone?" he asked.

I looked at him and hesitated, unsure whether or not to tell him about Yellow Thunder.

Before I had made up my mind, Cloud said, "Flint told me

62

about Yellow Thunder. I'm sorry, Cry. You'll get over him. There will be someone else someday."

"No," I whispered, "there will never be anyone else."

"Cry, would you like to go hunting? Maybe we could get some fresh meat for you before I go back to Oregon. I have my bow in the back of my truck."

"I'd like that!"

We stopped at my apartment, and I changed my clothes, and we were on our way to the high mountains.

I walked quietly behind Cloud as he moved like a shadow through the thick forest. The smell of pine and damp earth was thick in the cool air. Cloud was the best hunter and trapper I had ever known, but he would never kill an animal for sport. He loved the wild creatures and took only what he needed for food.

Cloud crouched near a fallen log and pointed to a small buck grazing on the side of the hill. He pulled his bowstring tight, took careful aim, and let the arrow fly to its mark. The arrow flew silently through the air and found its way to the deer's heart.

Cloud walked over to where the deer had fallen and spoke the ancient words, "Forgive me, my brother, my family must eat." He hesitated and looked at me. "I'm a Christian now. Is it wrong to still call the deer my brother?"

"I don't know. I don't see anything wrong with it. I think God meant us to feel close to animals. But—" I added, "but not like we used to in the old days, when we thought some animals were gods."

Cloud nodded, and I knew he remembered the time he had worshiped the eagle and bear gods. He bent over and began skinning the deer.

"Do you need the hide?" I asked.

"No, I won't want it. You can have it." He stood back, and I took his place beside the deer, skinning it with my hands instead of a knife because I wanted the hide for a dress and didn't want knife marks on it. After I was finished, I rolled up the heavy hide and dragged it to the truck while Cloud struggled with the deer.

After Cloud left for Oregon I felt more alone than ever and spent as much time at the church and at Reverend McPherson's home as I could. I knew that at times I overstayed my welcome and that I came at mealtime too often, but I didn't know what to do with myself. My hours were long and empty.

Audrey and Reverend McPherson may have groaned when they heard my knock at their door, but they were too kind to let me hear them. They always welcomed me and put an extra plate on the table.

I changed jobs again and worked in a greenhouse, but my thumb was red, not green, and plants seemed to just look at me and curl up and die.

Once again I sat in Reverend McPherson's study and announced I was unemployed.

"Crying Wind, soon you will hold a world record for changing jobs!" he scolded gently. "What are we going to do with you?"

"I'm lonely. Now that Cloud is gone again and Flint is married and Kansas is dead, I feel like the last of the Kickapoos."

"You need a cause, a calling, something you believe in that would add richness and purpose to your life," he said.

"Any ideas?" I asked.

"No, I'm sorry, you'll have to find your own calling. But I'll pray about it," he promised, and I left.

64

The following morning I found a job as a cook's helper in an Italian restaurant, and I called Reverend McPherson. "Do you think my life's calling could be making spaghetti?" I asked.

He laughed and said he didn't think so, but he was glad I had a job.

After work that day I was walking home, and as I stood on a street corner waiting for the light to change to green I noticed a scrap of paper in the gutter. It had the word *Navajo* written on it.

I picked it up and brushed it off and read that a Navajo mission in New Mexico needed workers.

I knew this wasn't an accident. God had planned this just for me! He had put that paper in the gutter and had made the light red so I would see it while I waited. I was sure of it!

I went straight to see Audrey and Reverend McPherson.

"How is the spaghetti maker?" Audrey asked.

"I'm going to quit," I said, and ignored their protests as I smoothed out the piece of paper and handed it to them, "I've found my calling. It's God's will for me," I said confidently.

They looked at the paper and handed it back. "What is this?" they asked.

"It says a mission in New Mexico needs workers," I explained to them, as if they couldn't read. "That's me! I'm going there to work!"

"Where did you get this?" Audrey asked.

"I found it in the gutter while I was waiting for the traffic light to change. God put it here for me."

"It could have been there for weeks." Reverend McPherson looked at the dirt on it. "What mission is this? Who supports them? What do they believe?"

"I don't know. I'll write to them today and say I'll come."

"Crying Wind, you have to think this over. It could be a cult or who knows what!" Reverend McPherson protested.

I folded up my precious piece of paper and left. I knew it was my calling, but it would take time to convince the McPhersons.

That night I realized what a big change had come over me since I had become a Christian.

Years ago, when we had heard about the five missionaries killed by the Auca Indians, we had laughed. We were glad they had been killed. Those missionaries had asked for it; they had it coming! They deserved to die. After all, what the Indians believed was their business. Those missionaries didn't have any right to butt in where they weren't wanted! We were glad the Indians had killed them, and we joked about it. We recalled that our tribe had killed many missionaries and had cut their heads off. We had been proud of that fact.

Now I wanted to work with missionaries to tell Indians about Jesus. Only God could have brought about that kind of change in my heart.

I wrote to the mission that night and explained that I was a Christian Indian and would come if they wanted me.

I waited on pins and needles until the answer came one week later. The missionaries asked me to come!

I almost ran to the church to show Reverend McPherson and Audrey the answer. "I'm going to work in a mission for Navajo Indians!" I shouted.

"What kind of mission? What is their doctrine? Who are they?" came the questions.

"I don't know." I shrugged. "I said I'd come, and they said OK."

Audrey rubbed her forehead as if it ached, and Reverend McPherson stared at me as if he thought I was losing my mind.

They argued for hours, but my mind was made up. In the end, Reverend McPherson loaned me a dozen books on prayer, doctrine, and devotions to take with me, and Audrey slipped twenty dollars into my pocket.

Once again we were saying good-bye, but it wasn't so painful this time, because I knew God's hand was in it.

I left on the midnight bus and rode five hundred miles to New Mexico. I was full of confidence and happy to have such a wonderful adventure ahead of me.

It wasn't until the bus door swung open and I stepped off and saw the mission truck waiting for me that I panicked.

Chapter Seven

A large man with a friendly smile came up and shook my hand. "Hello and welcome," he said.

I froze and my mind went blank. The only words I could remember were words I had heard my uncles say so many times. "Hi, honey!"

The missionary turned scarlet.

I bit my lip. "I'm sorry! I'm so nervous—I don't know why—I'll just get back on the bus and go home—" I stammered.

He began to laugh and picked up my bag and helped me to the truck, which had the name of the mission painted on its side.

Reverend Bell introduced me to his wife, Lola, and we began the long, dusty drive to the mission.

The missionaries asked many questions, and my answers were a disappointment to them.

"You are younger than we expected. How old are you, Crying Wind?"

"I don't know."

"What Bible college did you attend?"

"None, but I've read most of the Psalms."

"What education do you have?"

"None worth mentioning."

Reverend Bell went into a fit of choking.

Lola smiled nervously. "How long have you been a Christian?"

"A few months."

Her smile trembled and she simply said, "Oh."

Reverend Bell was once again in control. "What church is sponsoring you?"

"None. I just came on my own."

"But you said in your letter you spoke Navajo," Lola said encouragingly.

"Well, I used to, but I've forgotten a lot. I think I can pick it up again."

Reverend Bell turned red but remained silent.

Luckily we arrived at the mission soon after that. It was a brown adobe building with many rooms and had a chapel beside it. I fell in love with it at first sight. It was old and run down, but to me it was beautiful.

The sun went to bed and covered the sky with his red blanket. I unpacked and put my things away in my small room. Then Reverend Bell and Lola and I walked around the mission grounds.

I felt great peace in my heart, and knew it was God's plan for me to be here. Now it was up to God to convince Reverend Bell and Lola!

For the first time I was dealing with Christian Indians, and it thrilled my heart. The hours were long and the work was hard, and since I had come on my own, without support of a church, I received no pay. Once a week Audrey sent a letter and five dollars for my personal needs. I was working fourteen hours a day every day and getting five dollars a week, and I had never been happier.

I liked Lola and Reverend Bell, and they treated me as one

69

of the family. I helped Lola with the cooking and housework and other chores and taught Bible verses in English and Navajo. Several times a week we would go around the reservation and visit the Navajo families in their hogans.

One day Lola wasn't feeling well and didn't want to travel the eighty miles through the hot desert and bumpy roads to visit the settlements, so Reverend Bell and I went together and left Lola at the mission to rest. We had the truck loaded with clothes to give the women and candy for the children.

We had just left the first family, when Reverend Bell decided to cut across country and save ten miles instead of going down the road.

We hadn't gone far when he drove through a pile of tumbleweeds. He found out too late that the tumbleweeds were hiding a deep ditch, and we felt as though the world dropped out from under the truck. We sailed through the air and hit the bottom of the ditch so hard that we both bumped our heads on the roof of the truck.

When the dust settled, we climbed out of the truck and looked for damage. We had one flat tire, and a hole was poked in the gas tank. We plugged up the hole the best we could with a stick and changed the tire.

After several tries, Reverend Bell drove the truck back up the steep ditch and we were on our way once again.

We had gone only a few miles when the truck choked, gasped, and died. Reverend Bell turned the key several times, trying to start it, but it only groaned.

"We're out of gas," he said. "It's only a couple of miles to Old Mustache Woman's house. We can get help there."

When we got out of the truck the heat hit us like a giant fly swatter and almost knocked us to the ground. It was hard to breathe, and our eyes watered from the glaring white sun. Walking through the sand was slow, we were hot, and our mouths were too dry to talk.

I walked ahead of Reverend Bell, and when I looked back I saw he had dropped far behind me. As I sat down beside the road to wait for him, I noticed a beer can a few feet away. I picked up a pebble and threw it at the can. The pebble hit it with a dull clank. The can was not empty. I reached over and picked it up and shook it vigorously. The can had not been opened and was full of beer. It must have fallen out of someone's truck.

Reverend Bell walked up beside me. "What have you got there?" he asked, looking at the can in my hand.

"It's a full can of beer. I found it lying here in the sand." I handed it to him.

He looked at it and said, "I think I'll remove temptation from someone and pour this out in the sand, where it can do no harm." He grabbed the ring and yanked it off. At the same instant he was sprayed by a fountain of hot beer! He threw the can as far as he could, but the damage was done. He was soaked from head to foot and smelled like a brewery.

He looked at me with a red face and beer foam on top of his head.

I burst into shrieks of laughter and sat down on the sand and giggled helplessly. He stomped away across the sand, leaving me behind wiping tears from my eyes and laughing hysterically!

I thought it would be wise to walk behind him. It was better for him to think the hot sun had made the beer explode rather than my shaking the can to see if it was full!

The hot sun had dried out his clothing by the time we reached Mustache Woman's house, but the odor of beer lingered.

The dogs began barking as we approached the hogan. A gray, bent old woman pulled aside the blanket that served as a door, and she stepped outside.

"Yah'a'teh," she said.

"Yah'a'teh," said Reverend Bell, and he began telling her our reason for being there.

She said her son would be back soon with his truck and he would give us a ride back to the mission. While she spoke she kept sniffing the air and giving Reverend Bell suspicious looks, which he tried to ignore.

As we stood talking beside the hogan I noticed a bucket of water sitting on a stump. My tongue was stuck to the roof of my mouth. I nudged Reverend Bell and nodded toward the bucket of water.

Mustache Woman reached into her pocket and drew out a piece of black chewing tobacco and bit off a chunk with her few remaining teeth. In the next instant I knew how she had gotten her name. Tobacco juice streaked around her mouth and ran down her chin, making her look as if she had a mustache and beard.

She reached over and picked up a metal dipper and filled it with water from the bucket and offered it to me. I looked at her mouth and decided I wasn't as thirsty as I had thought I was. I couldn't bring myself to drink from her dipper.

She offered the dipper of water to Reverend Bell, and he took it and held it in his hands. He looked once again at the tobacco juice running down her chin, and then he looked back at the dipper. Thirst won the battle, and he took the dipper and turned it sideways. He drank awkwardly from exactly where the handle was attached, thinking that by drinking there his mouth would not touch where hers had.

The old woman laughed and slapped her knee and cackled, "Reverend Bell! You drink from the dipper the same way I do!" Then she spat.

Reverend Bell turned pale and sat down in the shade of a mesquite bush to recover.

He wiped his face with his handkerchief and said, "Crying Wind, I wondered why the Lord chose to send you to us, and today I found out. The Lord, in His wisdom, has used you to teach me humility today. When I became a minister I swore liquor and tobacco would never touch these lips. And thanks to you—"he glared at me—"I've been introduced to both vices in an hour!"

The ride back to the mission was silent except for the few times I couldn't hold back a small giggle.

After Reverend Bell recovered from his brush with alcohol and tobacco we had many laughs about our adventure. Whenever anyone mentioned the sin of pride, Reverend Bell would laugh and say, "Turn Crying Wind loose—she can make a person very humble very fast!"

After I had been at the mission one month a second volunteer worker arrived. She was a pretty blond girl with one year of Bible college behind her, and she felt she was being called to be a missionary. I eagerly awaited her arrival, because as much as I liked the Bells, I welcomed having someone near my own age.

Sharon was energetic and eager to win souls. The daily drudgery of kitchen chores and laundry rubbed against her grain. She wanted to be in the field spreading the gospel, not up to her elbows in dirty dishes.

At last her day came. Reverend Bell, Lola, Sharon, and I rode in the truck across the desert to visit a Navajo settlement twenty miles away.

"I'm so excited!" Sharon was bubbling with enthusiasm. "How many do you think will get saved today?"

"Probably none. Saving a soul is as rare as rain in the desert. It takes patience. Last year I saw only five people come to the Lord," Reverend Bell answered.

Sharon was more determined than ever to bring someone to God that day.

We parked the truck and walked into the Navajo camp. A Navajo woman with a half-dozen children clinging to her motioned us into her hogan.

The heat inside made it like an oven, and we had a hard time breathing. The Navajo woman and children crowded into one half of the hogan, and we sat in the other half, forming a circle on the dirt floor. The smell of the children's unwashed bodies hung heavy in the hot summer air.

The Navajo woman served us each squaw bread and a cup of stew. Sharon looked at the thick grease floating on top of her stew and whispered, "What do you think is in this?"

"Never ask!" I whispered back and took a bite. "It tastes a little like—" I looked around. "I wonder what happened to that old, gray cat they had?"

Sharon choked on her last mouthful of stew and turned pale.

"I was about to say, it tastes like mutton," I finished.

Sharon pointed at the only decoration inside the hogan. "What's that?" she asked.

It was a long, black, horse's tail, which the Navajo woman used as a comb holder. It looked for all the world like a scalp.

"I don't want to talk about it," I whispered, and Sharon's eyes grew wide.

At the same instant the Navajo woman spoke several words and pointed at Sharon.

Reverend Bell said, "Sharon, she just said your hair is like sunshine and she likes it very much."

Sharon put both hands on top of her head, scrambled to her

74

feet, and ran to the mission truck, where she remained behind locked doors until it was time to leave.

As we drove away from the camp she finally stopped holding her hair. "Nobody told me Indians stink!" she said, on the verge of tears. "Those heathens!"

"They only get one quart of water per day per person from their shallow well. They need it to drink, not to waste on washing. They smell like dust and campfire smoke and sagebrush. You smell like toothpaste, deodorant, perfume, hair spray, and powder. They think you smell funny," Reverend Bell explained.

Before we reached the mission we ran into a dust storm that left us choking and rubbing our eyes and scratching our itchy skin.

Sharon began scratching her head. Her hair spray had acted as a dust magnet, and her scalp was becoming irritated. The more she scratched, the more she itched.

"What a horrible day!" she groaned as we drove onto the mission grounds. "I feel so dirty! I can't understand what's making my head itch like this!"

"I hope it isn't lice," I said dryly. "You know how dirty those heathens are."

Sharon screamed, "Lice! I've got lice!" and she jumped out of the truck before Reverend Bell shut off the engine. Before we got inside the house she was washing her hair in the shower. A half-hour later she was still in the shower.

"Maybe you should go tell her it was just the dust making her itch," Lola suggested.

"She probably wouldn't believe me. After all, I'm 'one of them,' " I said.

Lola knocked on the bathroom door and finally convinced Sharon to come out.

"I'll never marry a missionary!" Sharon yelled. "I'm going to

75

marry a minister who has a nice, quiet, civilized church in the middle of Los Angeles!"

Two days later she packed and left, just before we were ready to visit another Navajo camp.

I missed her, and I felt guilty after she left. I knew I could have made things easier for her. I really shouldn't have teased her about the horse's tail hanging in the hogan. How was I to know she believed Indians still scalped people? I hoped she would find her minister and that he would have a big city church. She would be a good minister's wife. I was sure she would have some interesting tales to tell her children about the two weeks she spent among the "savages"!

We would rejoice when Indians came to Christ, and we would weep when we saw nearly half of them return to the old ways, going to the medicine man and ancient ceremonies and turning their backs on Jesus.

One day Blue Glass, a woman we considered our most faithful Christian, came to the mission asking for clothes.

"What happened to the clothes we gave you last week?" Lola asked.

Blue Glass looked at the floor and explained that she had washed them and hung them out to dry, and a dust devil had swept through them. Now they had little devils in them, and she was afraid to even take them off the clothesline. She was going to pay the medicine man a sheep to come take all the clothes down and burn them for her, to protect her from the dust-devil spirits.

Lola sighed and gave her some more clothes. "Do we ever reach them?" she asked tiredly. "Do we ever really reach them?"

Pony Boy Chee was a young warrior who caused more trouble than anyone in the area. He let air out of the tires of the mission truck, threw rocks at our windows, and threatened to burn the mission down. When he stole a horse belonging to the medicine man, everyone waited anxiously to hear the outcome, because the medicine man put a curse on him. He said that Pony Boy Chee would be burned up like dry grass.

Reverend Bell was aware of the constant battle between demonic power and the power of Christ, and he decided to use that as the topic for his sermon on Sunday. He said that although the evil power of the devil was very real, he didn't really believe the medicine man's curse would come true and that Pony Boy Chee, being the stinker he was, would probably live to a ripe old age.

That same Sunday afternoon, Pony Boy Chee was caught trying to rob a grave on the sacred burial grounds, and he was arrested by the Navajo police. As they were driving him into town to jail, a sudden thunderstorm blew up and rain came down in such heavy sheets the Navajo police were forced to pull the car off the road and wait out the storm.

Pony Boy Chee saw his chance and jumped out of the car and started to run. He hadn't gone a hundred yards when a bolt of lightning struck him and killed him on the spot. The police said his handcuffs must have attracted the lightning. The medicine man just smiled a lot and took advantage of his new power over those who believed his curse on Pony Boy Chee had come true.

I loved working at the mission and was very fond of Lola and Reverend Bell but many things troubled my heart about the way the mission was managed.

When clothes arrived for the Indians, Lola carefully went through each box and barrel and picked out the best of everything for Reverend Bell and herself. I learned that many missionaries did this, even though most poorly paid missionaries earned at least $8,000 a year and the average Indian family of six earned $1,000 a year at that time. Surplus clothes were stored in boxes in an old wooden shed.

"Why can't we just give out all the clothes as soon as they arrive?" I asked.

"The Indians don't appreciate them as much. It's better to dole out a little at a time," they would answer. I could understand that one shouldn't overwhelm a family with excess clothing; but I couldn't understand why Indian families had to freeze while dozens of boxes of good clothing sat in a dirty shed and molded or were eaten by mice and moths. Eventually they had to be burned because they were ruined.

Ladies' groups from many churches sent quilts for the Indians, but once again the missionaries didn't give them away freely. An Indian woman had to earn a quilt by coming to church six Sundays in a row. So her family shivered during the cold nights until she earned her quilt by walking many miles in all kinds of weather to meet her required six Sundays. If she came five Sundays and missed the sixth, she had to start all over again. It seemed hopeless, and quilts were stacked up in the storage shed while children slept cold.

"We can't let the Indians use us or take advantage of us," Reverend Bell would scold when I complained about the policies. "And be sure to keep all the doors locked. You know how Indians steal," he would say, forgetting that I, too, was Indian.

There was no record of anything ever being stolen from the mission. Indians, on the whole, do not steal. If an Indian does take anything it is nearly always food or an animal that can be butchered and eaten.

Reverend Bell was not the only one who made such sad mistakes in dealing with the Indians. Nearly every missionary in the area was equally guilty. They were all white people dealing with the red man, whom they didn't understand at all. Nearly half of the missionaries couldn't speak a word of Navajo, and several missionaries were just killing time until the doors opened to a more glamorous mission field in China or India or South America. The Bells had wanted to serve in Africa but had been turned down and had taken the Navajo as second choice. They never got over their disappointment, and it showed in their attitude.

After a year with the Bells I could see the mission system would never change until Indian preachers had their own missions. The white man could never reach the Indian as long as he looked at him as inferior, untrustworthy, and childish. The sheds filled with rotting clothing and quilts bothered me, and my heart broke over the way the missionaries treated the Indians.

I didn't want to leave the mission, because I loved the Indian Christians, but I was too restless to stay, and I knew it was time to move on. I had grown in my Christian life; it had been good for me to be in Christian surroundings for a year. I would always remember these days as happy times, and I remained friends with Reverend Bell and Lola in spite of our differences over mission policies.

My last night at the mission I stood motionless and looked out across the desert at the red sun sinking into the sand. Now it was only a scarlet sliver, and in another second it would be gone. I felt so lonely I wanted to cry. I could hear Lola and Reverend Bell talking in the house, man-and-wife talk about had she remembered to pay the light bill? and did he notice the cat was going to have kittens? Small, unimportant things, but things that weave two lives together.

Would I ever have anyone to share small talk with? I doubted it. What did I have to offer anyone? My family called me Double Ugly because I was twice as ugly as anyone else. No man would marry a girl called Double Ugly. I wished that somehow I could become beautiful. I kept waiting to "bloom" like other girls did, but instead of blooming I seemed to be wilting on the vine. I wasn't going to get any better looking; there was no Cinderella story for me. I cringed when I looked into the mirror. If only I had one good feature I could make the most of—but I didn't, and my uncles had been right, I was Double Ugly.

"God—"

I almost asked why didn't you make me pretty? But there wasn't much point to that, so I just said, "Don't let me want things I can't have. I know I'll never have a home or a husband or a family, so teach me not to want them, and show me how to be satisfied with only You."

I felt guilty as I walked back up the dusty trail to the mission for the last time. God should be enough for anyone. Why did I want more? After all, it wasn't so long ago that I had nothing. Was I just greedy? Would anything ever satisfy me?

Chapter Eight

It was a joyful homecoming when I returned to Audrey and Reverend McPherson. We talked for hours and tried to catch up on a whole year in one day. Once again, I stayed at their home until I could find a job and an apartment.

I looked up my Uncle Flint and found he had a baby son. Cloud also was married and had a baby daughter. They both seemed content with their new lives, and they were both becoming dedicated Christians.

A home, a wife, and a baby had put a smile on Flint's face. He was working hard at a steady job and had made many plans for his son's future. He was at peace with God, himself, and the world at last.

I took a job selling stationery and cards. It was easy work, and I liked the people I worked with. I made a new friend named Daisy, who was also a Christian, and we spent a lot of time laughing and sharing and praying together.

I felt as if everyone in the world were married except me. I read books on how to be single and happy, books on living alone, and even books on how to catch a husband, but nothing helped.

I spent hours talking to Reverend McPherson, and every conversation sounded the same.

"I'm lonely," I would begin.

"I know," he would answer.

"I want to get married," I continued.

He smiled. "Just getting married won't cure loneliness. Some of the loneliest people I know are married."

"Anything would be better than this," I shrugged.

"No, you're wrong. You could be a lot worse off. Believe me, a dozen people come to my office every week who are trapped in unhappy marriages and would give anything to be single again."

I nodded. I knew he was right. I knew many unhappy married women.

"You're young. It's a natural instinct to seek out a mate; you're hearing the 'call of the wild.' Be patient. If you make a mistake now, it could ruin the rest of your life."

"I don't suppose you know any half-breed who is looking for a squaw to keep his tepee warm?" I meant it as a joke, but it came out flat, and he didn't smile.

"Do you want to marry a—a man who is half Indian and half white?" He always refused to use the term *half-breed.*

"I don't know who else would have me. A full-blood Indian won't marry me."

"You wouldn't really want to go back and live on the reservation, would you?"

"No," I was quick to answer. There was too much poverty and hunger there. I would never go back. I didn't want to live in a one-room shack with a dirt floor. I wanted a real house, with electricity and water.

"You must marry a Christian man. Be sure he is a Christian before you marry him, because there's very little chance he'll change his ways after you're married."

"I've got to find him first," I said.

"Don't be in a hurry. He might be right around the next corner." He paused. "Or maybe God wants you to remain single."

"He must, or He wouldn't have made me look this way!" I complained.

"Crying Wind, you aren't an old maid! You are still very young. You have time to look around and make sure you get the right man. Let God guide you."

"That's easy to say. You aren't alone; you have Audrey."

"Yes, that's true. Sometimes it's too easy to give advice." He was quiet awhile and then he said, "Just don't get hurt." And the name *Yellow Thunder* hung unspoken in the air.

I walked back to my apartment, shut the door behind me, and stood in the darkness. Loneliness like winter frost filled every part of my body and left me cold and shivering.

It would soon be Valentine's Day. How I hated Valentine's Day! It was a screaming reminder that I was alone. I had never had a Valentine and probably would never get one.

I placed the Valentines on the card rack. Stupid cards! I picked one up and started to place it in the display rack and then hesitated. It was such a beautiful card. It had a huge red heart on it and said, "For you, darling, all my love, all my life." I held it in my hands and studied it, reading the verse over and over. On an impulse I put it in my purse and paid for it when Daisy wasn't watching.

That night I placed it on my table and looked at it as I ate my dinner. How I wished I would get a real Valentine someday. What a difference a silly piece of paper with a heart on it could make!

Daisy dropped in to visit, and soon she noticed the Valentine sitting on the table. She picked it up.

"Oh, Crying Wind, it's so pretty! Who is it from?" She opened the card. "It's not signed!"

I held my breath.

83

"A secret admirer!" she gasped. "How exciting! Do you know who it is?" She put the card back on the table.

I wanted to let the matter drop, but Daisy was too good a friend to deceive.

"I bought it for myself," I confessed.

"Me and my big mouth," she apologized.

After she left I took the Valentine, looked at it one more time, and threw it into the trash. I hated Valentine's Day!

The months dragged by. I thought of only one day at a time and never allowed myself to think of the future. I never missed church, but I had lost some of the joy I had known when I had first found God.

The skies always looked stormy, and there was always a gray wind blowing. There was no color in my world.

Chapter Nine

The store was being remodeled and we were given three days off. I was planning to sleep late and do a lot of reading, but the phone rang early and woke me up from a sound sleep. It was Daisy calling about a picnic.

"I don't want to go. I'm too tired," I yawned. "I'll go next time."

"No, we're counting on you. You'll wake up as soon as we get up in the cool mountain air. We'll be by to get you in fifteen minutes. Be ready." She hung up.

I hung up the phone and snuggled back down in bed. I could go back to sleep, and when she came I would ignore her. My eyes blinked back open. I couldn't ignore Daisy; she would bang the door down until I answered. I might as well get up. I would go this time, but never again. I felt irritable. I was tired. The last thing I wanted to do was go on a picnic up in the mountains. I pulled on an old pair of patched jeans and an old, faded shirt that had belonged to one of my uncles. I barely got a brush through my hair before I heard a horn honk outside. I practically staggered out to the car and flopped into the back seat beside two other girls.

"I'm sleepy," I mumbled. Daisy and her uncle and the other girls laughed and joked while I looked out the window and wished I were back in bed.

"My Uncle Dan thought he'd come along and do some fishing while we were getting the food ready," Daisy said over her shoulder.

I shivered. A fisherman. The thought of fish made my skin crawl. To my people, fish were unclean and had the spirits of evil women in them. My people would never eat fish! This just wasn't my day.

After traveling over winding roads for an hour, we reached the high mountain pass, and Daisy said, "This is it! Everybody out." Everyone grabbed food and blankets, and Daisy's Uncle Dan grabbed his fishing pole and headed for the trout stream nearby.

I spread out a blanket for our table and helped put the food out.

It wasn't long before Daisy and her friends were standing on the rocks beside Dan and offering him suggestions on his fishing technique. I watched from a distance for awhile but became bored sitting by myself, so I headed down to the trout stream to join the others.

There was a lot of giggling and silliness as the girls teased Dan, and he took it good-naturedly. I found myself laughing at them and was beginning to be glad I had come along.

"Why don't you guys go help that fisherman over there and leave me alone so I can get down to some serious fishing?" he said, trying to get rid of us.

It was the first time I had noticed that there was another fisherman downstream. He was too far away for me to see him clearly, but I could tell he was young and tall and strong looking.

Daisy looked downstream. "We could go down and ask if he's caught anything and what he's using for bait." And with that she and the other girls headed through the willows and across the rocks toward the other fisherman.

I sat down on a rock and leaned against a tree and watched the water rush by.

Dan laid down his pole and said something about having to go back to the car for more bait, and I was left alone.

I looked at the fishing pole lying beside me. I had never been fishing. After all, why would I want to catch something I would never eat? No, fish were dirty and unfit to eat. Even though I was a Christian now and knew there were no evil spirits in fish, I still couldn't bring myself to eat one of them.

I nudged the fishing pole with my foot. What an odd thing, a string and a hook on a stick. It didn't look hard to use. I wondered why people made such a fuss about it.

I looked up toward the car. Dan was digging around in the trunk, with his back to me. The girls were nowhere in sight. On a sudden impulse I picked up the pole and held it in my hands. I stood up and dipped the hook into the water. Wouldn't it be funny if I caught a big fish! I smiled to myself. That would be a good joke on everybody! I would have to get the hook out in deeper water as Dan had. *Let's see, you push this little round thing, and then you toss the pole backward and let it go, and then the hook lands far out into the water.*

Something was wrong! The hook hadn't gone out into the water! I turned around and looked in back of me. I had flipped the hook up into the trees, and it was tangled around a small limb. I jerked it a couple of times, and the pole bent. I looked toward the car. Dan was sitting on the blanket and drinking a cup of coffee. He didn't see me. I pulled on the pole again. The string wouldn't budge! Panic set in. Why couldn't I leave well enough alone! Now I had probably ruined Dan's fishing machine and had made a fool of myself. I wondered if I could climb up the tree and get it untangled. No, this wasn't a climbing tree. What in the world was I going to do? I stood there looking up into the tree and didn't hear footsteps behind me.

"There aren't any fish up there," a man's voice said.

The pole slipped from my hand. I whirled around and found myself looking into two gray eyes set in a tough-looking face.

He reached up and untangled the fishing line from the branch and turned the little handle until it was all neatly wound up again. He handed the pole to me, and I let out a sigh of relief and laid it back where Dan had left it.

I could feel the gray eyes watching me, and I wished he would go away. Just then I heard Daisy and the other girls pushing their way through the bushes. Daisy appeared first, picking leaves out of her hair.

"Oh, I see you've met Don," she said. "We've invited him to have lunch with us." Daisy walked past us with the other girls close behind her. "Did he tell you he's from Alaska? He's just here on vacation," she said and started up the path toward the picnic.

I hurried after her and wondered if Gray Eyes was going to tell everyone he had rescued me, but he didn't mention it.

Uncle Dan and the fisherman and the girls talked easily about the mountains and fishing, but mostly the girls asked him questions about Alaska. It was easy to see he loved the wilderness of his northern home.

I sat on a corner of the blanket and tried to eat lunch, but every time I looked up from my plate, old Gray Eyes was watching me. I became too nervous to even swallow my food.

After we had cleaned up the food and dishes, Dan suggested we all walk up the hill and look at the waterfall. I fussed over folding up the blanket until I saw they all were well on their way up the hill. Then I followed far behind.

I didn't try to catch up with the others until they had reached the waterfall. They were talking about crossing the stream and climbing to the top of the cliff. There was a three-foot jump across the fast-moving water. Dan was the first to go, and he made it easily. Daisy was next, and she nearly lost her footing and had to scramble a bit to get on solid ground. The two girls jumped across to the other side, and Gray Eyes simply stepped across with his long legs. Now everyone turned and waited for me to follow. I stepped up to the edge of the rocks and looked down at the swirling water. I wasn't sure I wanted to cross the stream.

"Come on, Cry!" Daisy urged.

The Alaskan leaned out over the water and held out his hand toward me. "Here, take my hand. I'll help you across," he said.

I hesitated. I didn't want to take his hand, but I was afraid I was going to fall into the water if I didn't.

"Trust me. I won't let you fall," said the Alaskan.

I took a deep breath and held out my hand. Strong fingers curled around mine and pulled me across the water, but when I was safely on the other side they didn't let go. I started to pull away, but the grip was firm, though gentle, and Gray Eyes led me up the path to the top of the cliff. Only when we reached the top did he allow my hand to slip out of his.

Daisy and the girls were picking wild flowers, and Dan was sitting on a rock to catch his breath.

The Alaskan reached down and picked a columbine and held it for a minute.

"Can you talk?" he asked.

I nodded my head yes.

He smiled and handed me the flower.

"It's pretty," I said.

"So are you," he said softly.

I looked at him to see if he was making a joke, but he was not

The Alaskan

laughing. My heart sank to my toes and then climbed back up again. I backed away and walked over to stand beside Daisy for protection. When I looked back, he was talking to Dan and seemed to have forgotten about me.

Why couldn't he go back to his fishing and leave us alone. After all, it was our picnic, not his!

We took a different trail back to the car, and I stayed as far away from the Alaskan as I could. It wasn't until we were starting to get into the car that he caught up with me.

"Do you have a boyfriend?" he asked.

I shook my head no.

"Can I see you again?" he asked.

I looked around. Everyone was watching us, and I could feel my face getting red.

"Where do you live?" he asked.

Dan started the car.

Daisy couldn't stand the suspense and said, "Since you are new here, why don't you come to church Sunday? We'd be glad to have you. It's the little brick church on Thirtieth Street." Then she added, "Crying Wind never misses a service," and she giggled.

The Alaskan smiled at her. "Thanks. I'll see you Sunday."

I refused to look at him as we drove away. Instead I looked down at the wilting columbine that I still held in my hand.

Occasionally the girls would nudge each other with their elbows and giggle and say that Dan hadn't caught any fish but it looked like Crying Wind had caught a man. I was glad when they left me at the door of my apartment.

Later, when I was alone, I gently placed the flower between the pages of a book. I would remember the day when a stranger had called Double Ugly pretty.

Sunday morning as I walked to church I wondered if Gray

Eyes would show up. I found myself wishing he wouldn't. He made me uncomfortable. I didn't see him when I entered the church, and I felt relieved. Well, that was that; I'd never see him again.

I had hardly sat down when someone sat down beside me, and I looked up into the face of the Alaskan. My hands trembled as I held the hymnbook, and I stole quick glances at the man beside me. His face was hard and tough looking, and his jaw was square and firm. With his blond hair and gray eyes, he really was a "pale face." It was only when he smiled that his gray eyes twinkled and gave way to the warmth inside. He was tall and had broad shoulders. His hands were strong and covered with scars and callouses from years of hard work.

For the first time since I had started coming to this church I didn't hear the sermon, because my thoughts were on the stranger beside me.

As soon as the last *amen* was said we stood up to leave, and several people came over to meet "the man who sat beside Crying Wind." While he was busy talking to them I slipped out the other side of the pew and stood beside Audrey.

"Is he your boyfriend?" she asked with a smile.

"I don't know him; he's a friend of Daisy's," I shrugged.

"It's strange he didn't sit beside Daisy," she said. "Why don't you come and have lunch with us? You can bring your friend if you want to. We'd be happy to have him." She patted my arm and began shaking hands with some of the people.

Gray Eyes was beside me again. "Can I take you out to lunch?"

"No, I'm eating with someone. Thanks anyway."

He looked disappointed. "Can I see you later today?"

"I don't know when I'll be home," I said.

"That's all right, I don't mind waiting. Where do you live?"

I looked around for someone to come to my rescue, but every-

92

one was visiting. I gave him my address and hurried to where Audrey was waiting for me.

During lunch Audrey and Reverend McPherson had many questions about "the man who followed Crying Wind to church."

"I don't know him at all," I tried to explain. "He's a stranger here, and I doubt I'll ever see him again."

"Oh, I'm sure we'll see him again," Audrey laughed.

I was glad when the conversation turned to other things.

Chapter Ten

I'd been home nearly an hour and was painting a picture of a sunset when there was a knock on my door. When I opened it, I was once again face to face with Gray Eyes.

"Hi. I heard a man was supposed to bring flowers and candy when he came courting." He smiled and handed me a penny sucker and some sad-looking dandelions. "I wanted to bring you something, but I couldn't find a store open.

I didn't hear your car," I said.

"It needed some work done on it, so I left it at a garage and walked here from Red Rocks Park."

"That's five miles," I said.

"It didn't seem very far. Besides, I have the feeling I came two thousand miles to meet you." He followed me inside.

We spent the afternoon working on a jigsaw puzzle I had started earlier. I couldn't think of a single thing to talk about, and whenever he tried to break the long silences by asking me a question, I would answer either yes or no, and again we would sit in silence.

He slipped the last piece of puzzle into place and stood up and stretched. "I have to go pick up my car now. Would you like to go out tonight?"

I hesitated, wondering what in the world we could talk about on a date. Besides, I didn't own any "dress up" clothes or even a pair of shoes—only moccasins, which were old and worn.

"No, I guess not," I said.

"We could go anywhere you would like to," he said.

I stood there looking at the floor. "I can't think of anyplace."

"I'll come back for you in a couple of hours. We'll go out to dinner." Then he left.

I shut the door and said to myself, *I didn't say I would go out with you.*

After dinner Don walked me to my door, and while I fumbled in my purse for my key he said, "I'm going to marry you someday. I only have a few days left here, and then I'll have to go back to Alaska. But someday I'll come back and marry you."

I dropped my purse, spilling everything in it. "You are making a joke," I said.

"No." He shoved my things back into my purse and handed it to me. "No, it's not a joke. I think we were meant for each other. I think our meeting was arranged, and I knew the minute I saw you that you were the one for me." He grabbed me and kissed me. "I love you, Crying Wind."

As soon as I got my breath back I said, "I can't marry anyone who doesn't belong to my church."

"I'll join."

"You have to be a Christian," I argued.

"I am a Christian," he said.

"Why would you want to marry me?" I asked.

"Because I love you. I'll never be rich. I have to work with my hands, but I can give you a house and food and clothes, and I'll take care of you. I'll never lie to you, and I'll take you to church every Sunday."

"It's too fast. I can't think so fast," I said, trying to get my key into the lock. I was shaking so badly I kept missing.

95

"I don't have time to do things the right way. I can't court you and bring you presents. I'll have to court you after we're married. Look, I know you don't feel much for me now, but someday you will." He waited for me to speak.

"I'll think about it," I said and quickly slipped inside and shut the door.

I couldn't believe it! A man had asked me to marry him! He didn't care that I was a skinny, ugly half-breed!

I didn't sleep at all that night. Of course, it was silly to think of marrying a stranger. I didn't know anything about him. Besides, he wasn't the kind of man I wanted. I wanted to marry Yellow Thunder, but he didn't want me. What if this was my only chance to get married? What if I didn't marry this Don Stafford and I was an old maid and lived alone all my life? I couldn't be too choosy; after all, who did I think I was? I wasn't pretty or smart or rich. What did I have to offer? True, Reverend McPherson said I was worth more than a star, but I couldn't picture myself telling any man he was lucky to marry me because in God's sight I was worth more than a star!

Early the next morning Reverend McPherson called to tell me that my friend, Don Stafford, had seen him and asked to become a member of our church and that he would join on Sunday morning. I was too stunned to say anything.

Later that day the Alaskan came to see me. He brought a silver locket engraved, "All My Love, Don."

"Did you think about it?" he asked.

"Yes."

"Well?"

"I don't know," I answered.

"I understand. For all you know, I could be Blue Beard or Jack the Ripper."

"Who?"

"Never mind," he said.

"Thank you for the locket." I put it on.

"I bought something else—just in case." He handed me a small box.

I opened it and found two gold wedding bands. Why did white people think gold was pretty? To me, silver and turquoise would have been far more beautiful.

I felt tired. Tired of working, tired of being alone, tired of making decisions, tired of wondering about my future. "If you want me, I'll marry you." I sighed. What did I have to lose?

He grabbed me and picked me up so that my feet dangled at least a foot off the floor. I was sure my ribs would snap if he hugged me any tighter, and the only thought that raced through my mind was, *What have I done?*

That night I met Reverend McPherson in his office. "Don asked me to marry him," I said.

"What was your answer?" he asked.

"I said I would." I felt embarrassed.

"Do you love him?"

The silence was so heavy I could feel it. "I'm tired. I don't want to be alone anymore," I said almost in a whisper.

"I want you to be happy. Do you think you'll be happy with Don?" he asked.

"I don't know. He seems to be all right, and he doesn't think I'm too ugly to marry. I don't think I'll ever get another chance to get married."

"Did you pray about this and ask God's will for you?

"I prayed, but I didn't hear any answer," I admitted. I was silent and looked at the floor.

"Marriage is difficult even when two people love each other," Reverend McPherson said. "But it's the love that holds it to-

97

gether during the hard times. Without love—well—" He made a hopeless gesture with his hands.

"But he must want me, or he wouldn't have asked me to marry him. He could do a lot better than me, but I'm the one he chose. It's the first time anyone ever wanted me. Besides, what have I got to lose?" I argued.

Reverend McPherson groaned and shut his eyes. "Crying Wind! If you only knew! I can't tell you the heartbroken people who come here from unhappy homes."

"But I'm lonely!" I pleaded.

"But you might get married and still be lonely."

"Look, maybe this love business is overrated. Maybe people expect too much from love and they get disappointed. Maybe when you get married you shouldn't expect anything at all; then you won't be disappointed," I reasoned.

"What do you think your life will be like with Don?" he asked.

"I don't know. I'll keep his house and cook, and he'll provide food and shelter. It's a good deal."

"What about children?" he asked bluntly.

I blushed. "I don't want any."

"What does Don want?" he asked.

"I don't know. We didn't talk about it."

"Crying Wind! What are you doing with your life?" he demanded.

"My life hasn't been worth much so far. Maybe it will get better. All I know is that I don't want to be alone."

"But you aren't alone!" he said. "God loves you, we love you, you have friends in the church—"

"I know that, but every night I go home to an empty room, eat supper by myself, and spend my evening reading a book. I

98

know God loves me, but I want someone to talk to and be with. I want to get married," I said.

"That's it, isn't it. You didn't say 'I want to marry Don,' you just said, 'I want to get married.' " He sighed.

"Don asked me, and nobody else has, so he's the one I'll marry," I said stubbornly.

"For the rest of your life, till death do you part?" he asked. I refused to answer.

"Marriage isn't one of your jobs that you can quit after a week if you don't like it," he warned.

"I don't want to be alone," I repeated.

He rubbed his eyes as if he felt very tired. "I can see your mind is made up. I can't tell you how to live your life. I wish you would wait awhile, but if you won't, I would be proud to perform the marriage ceremony." He held my hand, "God bless you, Crying Wind, and God help you!"

I wrote to Cloud and told him I was getting married and that I would write again after I knew where I was going to live.

Next I told Flint.

"You're what?" he asked.

"I said I'm getting married."

He burst out laughing. "Are you serious?"

"Yes. I'm getting married in a few days." I swallowed hard and waited for the explosion I knew was coming.

"Who is it? You aren't even dating anyone!" he laughed.

"I met him a few days ago," I said.

"Who is he? Where is he from? What tribe does he belong to?" Flint asked.

"His name is Don Stafford. He's from Alaska." I took a deep breath. "He's white."

"He's white? You want to marry a white man? Are you crazy?" he yelled.

"He wants to marry me, and I said OK. He joined my church—" My voice trailed off.

"You know what they say about mixed marriages! Will your Mr. Stafford like being called a squaw man? You'll be called worse things than that. It will never work!" he said flatly.

"I've been called names all my life. You know that. Besides, I'm a half-breed, so that makes me half-white. Indian men don't want me. What do you expect me to do, wait for a half-breed to come along?"

"Your own mother was Indian and your father was a white man, and their marriage didn't last a month. That should prove something to you!" he said.

"They weren't Christians. Don and I are both Christians," I argued.

"You're making a terrible mistake!" He paced the floor. "Why are you doing it?"

"You should understand better than anyone, Flint. I'm lonely," I said simply.

"You're selling yourself!" he shouted.

"I'm getting married!" I shouted back.

"Not for love! You're not getting married for love!" he yelled more.

"What do I know about love? Who has ever loved me?" I answered.

"You'll be sorry! He'll leave you in a month for a white woman. You'll be left with a baby and no place to go, and you'll end up like your mother."

I didn't want to argue anymore. "Please come to my wedding, Flint."

"No!" he growled.

"I came to yours," I said.

"We married for love. It wasn't a business deal!" he snapped.

100

"Try to understand—"

"I do understand. You sold out!" He lowered his voice. "Why does he want to marry you?"

"I don't know," I answered truthfully.

"You'd better think about this. What is he after?"

I braced myself for the same lecture I had heard all my life.

"You're hard to look at, Cry. You have a big nose and crooked teeth, your ears stick out, and you're too skinny to have a figure. You aren't even a good cook. A man would have to be crazy to want you!"

"Maybe I'm marrying a crazy man." I'd had enough. "Look, Flint, he said he'd marry me, and, like you said, I can't be choosy. If he only keeps me a month, then at least I'll know somebody wanted me for a month. If I end up with a baby, then I won't be alone anymore. I have nothing to lose."

I left feeling worse than when I had come. Once again thanks to Flint, I was aware of every fault I had, and I wondered, *Why would the Alaskan want to marry me?*

The next few days flew by. We had just ended our fifth date, and Don walked me to the door of my apartment.

"Well, tomorrow is the day," I said. "If you still want to go through with it."

He smiled. "I love you," he said.

I knew I was supposed to say "I love you" back, but I couldn't, so I said "Thank you," and shook his hand. "I'll see you at church tomorrow." And with that I said good night to the man who was to be my husband the next day.

It was a cold, windy day. I woke up and felt fear spread from my heart down to my fingers, which were shaking so badly I couldn't hold a cup of coffee without spilling it.

Today is my wedding day. Today I'm going to marry Don Stafford from Alaska, I said to myself.

"Oh, no I'm not!" I answered and walked outside slamming the door behind me.

I went to a nearby riding stable and rented a horse.

Wedding Day

"How long will you be gone?" the stable owner asked.

My wedding was set for two o'clock. "I'll be back at four o'clock," I said. I kicked the horse in his sides and galloped off toward the mountains.

The horse was fat and slow, but at least it was a horse, and riding beat walking any time.

A good ride always lifted my spirits, but today the farther I rode, the worse I felt. I kept seeing Mr. Stafford standing there in the church and waiting for me to show up; people watching the door, waiting for me—

102

No. No, I bet Mr. Stafford wasn't going to show up, either. He wasn't really going to marry me; it had been a joke. I smiled. It would be funny. Wouldn't everyone be surprised when neither the bride nor the groom showed up for the wedding? That would sure be a first for Reverend McPherson! I wished I could see the expression on his face when he had to explain to the people that there would be no wedding because the bride and groom had both changed their minds!

But what if the Alaskan did show up? What if he was there now, waiting for me? How embarrassing for him, how humiliating! How cruel of me!

My heart felt sick. I would have to go back. I had said I would marry him; I would have to do it.

I turned the horse around and headed toward the stable. The air was growing colder, and my hands were stiff and clumsy as I guided the horse back down the trail.

It was ten minutes before two o'clock when I sneaked in the back door of the church and walked into the kitchen, where Sally and Audrey were putting out punch and plates.

Sally looked up. "Where have you been? You aren't even dressed! You have hay in your hair!" She flew around the edge of the table and grabbed my hand, and she and Audrey dragged me off to a small room where a borrowed wedding dress was waiting.

"Did he show up" I asked. "Is Mr. Stafford here?"

"Of course he's here! He's been here over an hour!" Audrey slipped the white lace dress over my head while Sally untied my moccasins and slid on some white shoes. "Where have you been?"

"I was horseback riding," I said.

"Horseback riding on your wedding day?" Sally looked up.

"I didn't think he would show up," I shrugged.

103

"Oh, for heaven's sake!" Audrey groaned. In a matter of minutes they had me dressed, the hay combed out of my hair, and a veil stuck on my head and were pushing me out the door.

They each gave me a quick "God bless you!" and a hug and disappeared into the sanctuary.

I looked over to the exit door. *Maybe I could just walk out that door and go home and—*

"Are you ready?" Reverend McPherson's voice made me jump.

"I guess so. Did any of my uncles come?"

"No," he said.

"I didn't think they would." I shrugged.

"You look beautiful. May I give the bride away?" He smiled and took my arm.

The music started, and we entered the sanctuary. When we stepped inside I saw all my friends from the church, and a lump came to my throat and tears stung my eyes. Up in front the candles were flickering on the altar, and there stood the Alaskan, watching me and smiling.

I was petrified throughout the ceremony and reception and moved like a robot, with a frozen smile on my face.

In less than an hour we were ready to begin our lives as man and wife.

There was a bad moment when it was time to sign the marriage certificate.

"I don't want to change my name. If I'm Mrs. Don Stafford, what happens to Crying Wind?" I asked.

"You aren't changing your name, you're adding a name. It only means you belong to somebody. Now you are **Crying Wind Stafford**." Reverend McPherson handed me the pen and I signed.

The car door slammed shut behind me and everyone stood

104

around the car waving and throwing rice. Audrey and Sally were crying, and Reverend McPherson looked worried. As the car pulled away, I realized again that I was going away with a stranger.

I glanced over at him. He didn't take his eyes off the road, but he said, "It's going to be all right. I promise you won't be sorry." He drove about a block and then reached into his pocket and pulled out an envelope and handed it to me.

"There's a hundred-dollar bill in there. Reverend McPherson gave it to me when we left and said it was from your friends at the church. You keep it; it's yours. Call it escape money, and if you are ever unhappy, you can take the money and come back to your friends."

I reached over and took the money and hid it in my purse. I felt better. *Escape money.* I liked that. Now I could leave any time I wanted to.

And so began my life as Mrs. Don Stafford. I was married to a quiet stranger I had known only a few days. I went to my marriage bed with tears in my eyes, fear in my heart, and the knowledge that I had married a man I didn't love while I still carried memories of Yellow Thunder in my heart.

Chapter Eleven

We were on our way. Miles flew under the wheels and were tossed away by the rear tires. A hundred miles, five hundred miles. In a few days we would be in Alaska, thousands of miles from my home and friends.

Would we live in an igloo? Did it snow all year? What if he decided he didn't like me and threw me out? I looked over at him. He was deep in his own thoughts. Was he sorry he had married me?

We stopped to eat, and he looked at the menu. "What do you want?" he asked.

"Nothing. I'm not hungry," I said. I was too frightened to eat or drink. I felt like a wild animal that had suddenly been thrown into a cage.

We crossed the American-Canadian border, and as I saw the American flag fade into the distance I was sure I would never see my home again. I was going to the end of the world.

I had eaten only a few bites of food since we had been married, but by the time we reached the Yukon, hunger won over everything else, and I began eating like a lumberjack—much to my groom's relief. The Yukon was the most rugged, beautiful country I had ever seen. We would drive for hours without seeing another car or house. The wildlife was thick, and we saw moose, fox and deer. Beside one lake we counted over a hundred bald eagles diving into the water to catch the small fish. Once we

106

stopped to explore a long-deserted Royal Canadian Mounted Police camp, and I saw a three-legged bear. Don grabbed me and we ran to the car while he mumbled something about a three-legged bear still being faster than a two-legged girl and how was he going to explain to Reverend McPherson that he had let a bear eat me!

It was late and we were both tired and hungry when we stopped at a small café one evening for dinner. We sat down in a booth and a waitress came to our table with one menu, which she handed to Don.

"I'm sorry, sir. We won't serve her here," she said.

Don looked up from the menu. "What do you mean?"

The girl jerked her thumb toward me and repeated. "We won't serve Indians. She'll have to leave." She pointed to a sign on the window.

Don's eyes were like cold steel as he handed the menu back to the waitress. He reached over and took my hand, and we left.

We drove in silence for several miles. Then I decided I'd better say something.

"It doesn't really matter. Let's just forget it."

"They're stupid!" Don spoke louder than he had to.

"I know. Shall we go back and scalp them?" I asked.

A smile broke the hardness of his face. "I'm sorry, Cry."

"It's harder for you. I've lived with it all my life," I said.

"Does that mean you are used to being treated like that?" he asked.

"No," I answered quietly. "No, you never get used to it; you just live with it."

Don had had his first taste of what it was like to be a "squaw man," and it had made him angry. I wondered if he would be able to take it, or if he would decide it was too hard and leave me for a yellow-haired woman.

We arrived in Alaska late one evening. The only room we could find was above a bar, and it cost fifty-two dollars for the night. The noise and brawling sounds filtered into our room as badly as the smell of whiskey and smoke. We both looked at the small, dirty room and then at each other.

"It's too cold to sleep in the car. This is the only room left," he explained. "I just hope those drunken Indians don't keep us awake all night—" His face turned red and he closed his eyes tightly. "I didn't mean that! I'm sorry! I wasn't picking on the Indians, I just meant that I hoped those people downstairs would settle down pretty soon and we could get some rest."

"It's all right," I said.

"I'll go see if I can get us some food. Be sure you lock the door, and don't open it until I tell you it's me."

"Don't let any Indians scalp you," I warned and locked the door behind him.

It was nearly an hour before I heard his knock.

"They didn't have any food downstairs so I had to walk to another place down the block, and it took them so long to cook it." He unwrapped some greasy hamburgers. "The Indians downstairs had a bear in the bar that one of them had killed today." He handed me a hamburger. "It isn't going to be like this, Cry. It isn't going to be dirty rooms and cold food for you. Don't judge our married life by tonight."

I suddenly felt sorry for him. He was trying so hard. It hadn't occurred to me until that minute that maybe he was scared to death, too. I had thought of him as older than myself because he had been so many places and done so many things. But now I realized that in spite of his adventurous life, he wasn't much older than I was.

He told me how he had left home when he was a teenager and had driven to Alaska, where he had worked as a fisherman on a crab boat. Then he had worked in the oil fields, where it was sixty-five degrees below zero. He told me of the years he had spent working in the cold wilderness, and I began to realize that he was lonely, too. He was so lonely that He didn't even know I was ugly.

"Marriage is a period of adjustment that lasts all of your lives," Reverend McPherson had said to us. He had given us a lot of advice, but when he had used the word *adjustment* he had just shown us the tip of the iceberg. As if it weren't enough of a difference that Don was a man and I was a woman, he was white and I was Indian, and we were from two different cultures—he was living in a modern, complicated world, and I still had one foot in the Stone Age.

The long trip had given me a terrible headache.

"Why don't you take something for it?" Don asked.

"I don't have anything here with me," I said, holding a cold washcloth over my eyes.

"I can go get you something. What did you use for a headache back on the reservation?" he asked.

"I put rattlesnake rattlers in my headband."

"You what?"

"That was the best cure. But if you couldn't find a rattlesnake then you could eat wild rose petals."

"I'll buy a bottle of aspirin," he said.

"Do you really think that will work?" I peeked out from under the washcloth.

"A lot of people use aspirins for headaches," he answered.

"Well, all right, I guess that will do until we can find a rattlesnake," I agreed.

That was only the beginning.

As soon as we arrived in Anchorage he rented a small cabin and bought supplies. He only had a few days before he would fly hundreds of miles away back to his job on an oil platform. He would be gone ten days and then be home five days.

I had mixed emotions about my new home. Living in the middle of Alaska was not what I had planned for my life, but it was what I had agreed to.

"Lord, help me!" I prayed.

Chapter Twelve

I cooked our first dinner—meat, potatoes, onions, corn, and fry bread—and set it on the table.

Don smiled at me and took a bite and chewed it a very long time. He started to take a second bite but instead he excused himself and left the room. In a few minutes he came back into the kitchen. He still had a smile on his face, but he was as white as a sheet.

"It's my cooking, isn't it? You can't eat my food," I accused, half-angry, half-ashamed. "I should have known a white man couldn't eat Indian food!"

"No, it's not that. It's just, well, I've never eaten an entire meal that has been cooked in one skillet all at the same time. It tastes—unusual," he explained.

"You hate my cooking," I sulked.

"No, really, it's fine. I'll get used to it." He sat back down and looked at the food floating across his plate in yellow grease. "Maybe if you used a little less grease? My potatoes keep slipping off my plate."

"Grease is good for you; it keeps bears away."

"There aren't any bears here," he said.

"See! It works!" I snapped.

"Don't you have any recipes?" he asked timidly.

I lit up. "Yes! I have a very good recipe."

111

"Good!" He was encouraged. "What do you need?"

"First you mix one quart of raw alcohol; one pound of rank, black chewing tobacco; one bottle of Jamaica ginger; one handful of red peppers; one quart of black molasses; and one quart of water; and then you boil it until all the strength is drawn from the tobacco and peppers, and you drain it and it's finished," I said proudly.

"What in the world does that make?" he asked.

"Kickapoo Trade Whiskey!" I answered eagerly.

"Is that the only recipe you know?" he asked.

"Yes." I had the feeling it was the wrong one.

"I'll buy you a cookbook." He shook his head. "That stuff probably killed more Kickapoos than all the wars in history."

"My uncles drank gallons of it. It didn't hurt them," I said, and watched a potato float across my plate in a river of grease.

"Your uncles must have cast-iron stomachs," he observed and scraped the food off our plates. He dug out three skillets and cooked eggs in one, bacon in another, and potatoes in the third. Soon we were eating a delicious meal. I had married a good cook. He did everything so well for himself, I wondered why he had married me.

After dinner I kicked the front door open, as I always had, and threw out the leftovers.

"Honey, you can't do that," Don said.

"Do what?"

"You can't throw garbage out the front door. It looks bad."

"What am I supposed to do with it? Back on the reservation we always threw it out the front door."

"But it's different now. Put it in the garbage disposal."

"What's that?"

He led me to the sink and shoved some food down the drain.

"So that's why the sink looks funny on one side." With a

spoon, I shoved the rest of the garbage into the hole in the sink and turned on the switch. The spoon was yanked out of my hand and disappeared down the drain with a terrible, loud, grinding sound.

Don reached over and flipped off the switch and pulled out a mangled spoon.

I looked at the spoon. "Seems to make more sense to throw garbage out the front door than to bend up all your spoons," I said and left the kitchen.

The first night in our new home I sprinkled a generous supply of cornmeal on the doorstep to insure that we would always have enough food to eat. Let people throw rice if they wanted to, but I would depend on cornmeal on the doorstep.

I had always been so quiet, so silent—seldom speaking, and moving through life like a shadow, remaining invisible and unnoticed in the background. I had been trained in the old way, a reminder of the days when silence meant survival. Silence kept you hidden from your enemies; silence helped you stalk a deer or trap a rabbit. Noise frightened away game, and you went hungry. Noise could get you killed. Now it was different. I had to learn to talk, to make unnecessary noise, to speak when there was nothing to say, to "make conversation."

It was hard to think of things to say to this stranger who knew nothing of life on the reservation or what it meant to be an Indian.

When Don would complain that I was too quiet I would answer, "We don't have anything in common to talk about."

I was surprised when Don suddenly seemed to know a great deal about Indian cultures. Every evening during dinner he would have something to say about one of the tribes or one of the great chiefs.

"I didn't know you knew so much about Indians," I said one evening after he had finished talking about Geronimo.

"Oh, yes, I've always been interested in Indians." He paused. "You were wrong, you know; you and I really do have a lot in common."

Something in his look was odd, but I couldn't put my finger on what it was.

It wasn't until late one evening that his little secret came out by accident. I was cold, and I remembered I had left my sweater in the car and went after it. As I reached into the back seat to get it, I saw the corner of a book sticking out from under the seat. I couldn't remember leaving a book in the car, but I knew it had to be mine, because Don never read books.

I pulled it out and found there were not one but three books stuffed under the seat. I read the titles.

The A to Z of American Indians—Apaches to Zunis
Battle of the Little Bighorn
The Red Man—The Noble Savage

I started to giggle. Thinking they would help him understand me, Don was secretly reading these books. When I looked at the title *The Noble Savage* I burst into laughter.

He had underlined parts of the books and memorized them almost word for word. I could remember his dinner conversations and could see they were straight from the books. I wondered how many hours he had spent sitting in the car and trying to read these dull, outdated books, as slowly as he read.

I stopped laughing. It wasn't really very funny at all. He was trying so hard to understand me. I was touched by how much he cared. Maybe I should try harder, too. I slid the books back into their hiding place under the seat and went inside. It would remain his secret.

114

Nightmares. Every night. Horrible dreams that made me wake up screaming, with my heart pounding so hard it shook my whole body. I had thought that after I became a Christian the nightmares would stop, my mind would no longer be troubled, and I would sleep peacefully; but the dreams had continued, and each night I dreaded going to bed. I knew that in the middle of the night my dreams would haunt me, and I would wake up frightened half to death.

One dream I had often was about Twice Blind, the medicine man whose family had cut his legs off when he died so that he wouldn't walk back from the grave and kill them. I dreamed over and over that he was crawling on his bloody stumps out of his grave.

In other dreams I was a child back in school again, with a hard-looking teacher punishing me for everything I did because it was wrong in her eyes. When the school day ended, gangs of children would chase me home, shouting names and throwing rocks. When I woke up and realized I was not a child and would never have to go back to school again, I would thank God. I was grown up now; I never had to go to school again. No one would chase me home and throw rocks at me; no more teachers would frighten me until I was sick to my stomach. No, I was safe from school.

Some nightmares were so bad I couldn't repeat them even to Don. I would wake up screaming and weak with fear. Too afraid to go back to sleep, I would get out of bed and sit in a chair and keep all the lights on the rest of the night.

It was time for our first separation; Don was flying away to work.

"I'll be back in ten days," he said, holding onto me at the airport. "It will go faster than you think. If you need anything, call the number I gave you, and my friend will help you." He kissed me good-bye and picked up his suitcase and climbed into the plane. In a few minutes the small plane was out of sight.

He's gone! He'll never come back! I'm alone here in a foreign country! I cried all the way home. Flint had been right; I'd been abandoned, just as he said I would.

I moped around for days and passed the long hours by reading books. Exactly ten days later Don burst through the door in a swirl of snow. "I'm home!" he shouted.

I ran to him and threw my arms around his neck. "You came back! You came back!" I couldn't believe it.

"I told you I'd be back in ten days. Why would I marry you and bring you all the way up here just to leave you? Won't you ever learn to trust me?"

The five days together slipped away fast, and it was soon time for him to leave again. Time was heavy on my hands when Don was gone and flew by quickly when he was in town. After each ten-day absence he would return, and each time I would wonder how many more times he would return before he left for good. I'd been abandoned too many times in my life not to expect it to happen again.

When I had lived alone there had been no sounds except my own. Now there were sounds in the house as he wound the alarm clock in the bedroom or emptied change from his pockets and put it on the dresser. Sounds of doors opening and closing, dishes rattling. Sounds of life. There was silence when he was gone, but it wasn't the deep, lonely silence I had known before, because I knew that when he returned the house would again have life in it.

NIGHT MUSIC

The night is still,
Except for the sound of love beside me,

116

A warm, familiar sound
That tells me I am not alone.
The burdens of the day are hidden by the darkness;
I drift far above the earth on a soft white cloud,
Taking only the echo of your presence with me.
The night is still,
Except for the sound of my husband snoring,
A warm, familiar sound
That tells me I am not alone.

"You haven't asked for anything since we've been married,"
Don said one day. "You need some things. Wouldn't you like
to go shopping and buy some new clothes or something?"

"Well—" I hesitated—"I would like a new dress."

"Great! How much money do you need?" He dug out his
wallet.

"Oh, I was going to make it myself," I said.

"All right, what do you need? I'll get it for you."

"Well, I need two elk skins and ten pounds of beads," I answered.

"What?"

"I want to make a new buckskin ceremonial dress," I explained.

He was silent for a moment and then his face lit up.

"There's a fur trader down by Boot Legger's Cove. Let's see
if he has some skins."

A short time later I had some deerskins and ten pounds of
beads and six rabbit skins that I had admired.

The next time Don returned from work the dress was nearly
finished.

"What are you going to do with the rabbit skins?" he asked.

"I drew on them with ink," I said and pulled my surprise out to show him.

He looked at my ink drawings of moose, caribou, and deer on the skins.

"They are a gift for you," I said shyly.

"They are really good! I like them." He studied them awhile. "Would you like to make some to sell?"

"No one would buy my paintings. I'm not an artist," I said.

"Let's buy ten skins, and I'll get you some paints and brushes. You make more pictures like these, and I'll sell them to the gift shops."

I laughed at him but painted the ten skins. He sold them to a gift shop the next day for seven dollars each and came home with an order for forty more pictures.

"This is your money," he said as he handed it to me. "You can make a lot of money with your paintings if you want to. Use the money for anything you want, but don't buy food or pay bills with it. I promised to support you, and I will. But if you enjoy painting and want to use the money to buy gifts for your friends or give it to your church, it's all right with me."

I nodded, too excited to speak. People were buying my paintings! During the next year Don sold over five hundred of my sketches and paintings, most of them on rabbit skins. I became so used to painting wild animals, I could paint thirty pictures in a day. Don had talked every gift shop within a hundred miles into carrying my pictures.

One day he said, "I think you should have your own checking account and keep your money from your paintings in it. Fill out this form and put your social security number on it and sign it Mrs. Don Stafford."

"Why can't I be Crying Wind?" I asked.

118

"People will think we aren't married," he answered.

I compromised and wrote "Crying Wind Stafford."

Don sighed. "Now fill in your social security number."

"I don't have a number, only a name," I said.

"Everyone has a social security number," he insisted.

"Not me."

"You've had a lot of jobs—you had to have a number," he argued.

"No. I just said I forgot it, and since I didn't work anywhere more than a few weeks nobody bothered me about it," I explained.

"We'll get you a number."

"I don't want a number! I'm Crying Wind. I have a name; I don't want a number. Numbers are bad luck. If you let the government give you a number, they can find you," I insisted.

"What's wrong with that?" he asked.

"Indians should never let the government find them," I said.

"Why not?"

"They might decide to exterminate all the Indians."

"That's ridiculous!" Don laughed.

"They tried it a hundred years ago. It could happen again," I argued. "Look what happened to the Jews in Germany!"

"You are an Indian living in the United States. I'll get a social security number for you." Then he laughed, "If the government comes looking for you, I'll hide you in the attic!"

"Sure, that's what you say now!" I said, frowning.

A short time later he showed up with an envelope with two social security cards in it. He took one out and put it inside the box where he kept his important papers and handed me the other card.

As Don left the room, I looked at the card. I was no longer

119

Crying Wind. I was number 522-54-2700. Now the government had me in their number machine. Now they could find me, and Don had probably lied about hiding me in the attic! I took the card and tore it into many small pieces and threw it into the wastebasket. There! Now I was Crying Wind again!

Don came back into the room. "By the way, you'll have to get an Alaskan driver's license. Let me have a look at the one you have now."

I dug out my driver's license and showed it to him.

"This says it belongs to Rose Begay Tsosie," he said.

"Yes, I know," I said, nodding.

"Where is your own driver's license?"

"That *is* mine. I bought it at the pawnshop."

"You can't get a driver's license at a pawnshop!" he laughed.

"Of course you can. On the reservation you can pawn your driver's license for fifty cents. That is enough to buy one drink at the saloon. Then if you can't get it back out of pawn, the pawnbroker sells it for two dollars."

"You can't do that!" Don exclaimed.

"Sure you can. All Indians look alike to the police—black hair, brown eyes, dark skin. All you have to do is buy one that reads close to your age and weight."

"You can't do that!" Don repeated, "That's illegal! Are you telling me that half the Indians in America are driving around using a license they bought in a pawnshop for two dollars?"

I shrugged.

Don went off mumbling to himself, and I put Rose Begay Tsosie's license back into my purse. I had never seen anyone so concerned about laws and rules.

After several heated discussions, Don took me down to the police station, where I got a legal driver's license.

"I don't see what difference it makes. I drive the same way whether I use this one or the one I bought in a pawnshop," I complained.

Don shook his head and sighed, "A man needs nerves of steel to be married to an Indian!"

Chapter Thirteen

It was the middle of the night when something woke me. When Don was gone I slept lightly and heard every little sound, and I knew something was wrong. I lay listening in the darkness for a few seconds, but when I didn't hear anything I concluded I must have been dreaming and decided to go back to sleep. I pulled the covers up around my shoulders and turned over in bed—and found myself face to face with a strange man!

I screamed and sent the blankets flying in all directions and was out of bed and running across the room in a split second. I started throwing everything I could find.

The red-bearded stranger sat up in bed and rubbed his eyes.

"What on earth is wrong with you, Cry?" It was Don's voice, but it was coming out of someone else's face.

I took a couple of steps closer.

"I got a chance to come to town a day early but it was so late I decided not to wake you. I didn't mean to scare you," he apologized.

"What happened to your face?" I couldn't believe this hairy man was my husband.

"Oh, us guys decided to grow beards," he laughed. "Do you like it?"

"You have hair all over your face! You scared me to death!" I put down the bookend I was holding. "You aren't supposed to change your face when I'm not looking!"

I put the blankets back on the bed and found my pillow across the room, where I had thrown it in the confusion, and I settled back down for the night. Indian men don't have hair on their faces; if you marry an Indian you know he will always look the same—he isn't going to grow a beard or get bald.

"The next thing I know he'll be bald," I grumbled under my breath.

"What's that?" Don asked sleepily.

"Nothing." I answered and reached over with one finger and touched the red beard. "Good night, fur face."

The next morning as I was getting dressed I took a good look at myself in the mirror. I looked as if I had just come off the reservation.

I decided that since I had a new life now, I should look different. I should conform to the way other women dressed so I wouldn't embarrass my husband.

I went shopping and bought a street-length dress, but after wearing long dresses all my life I felt half-naked with my legs hanging out. Besides, they were cold. The panty hose the clerk had sold me did everything but keep my legs warm. They sneaked up and they sneaked down and they moved around more than I did.

PANTY HOSE

Are you some strange jungle beast
Whose savage nature has been released?
Writhing and crawling all around,
Then sneaking up without a sound—
Panty hose, I beg you, please,
Don't twist and sag around my knees!

123

The New Me

Next came the beauty parlor. I took a deep breath and walked through the door, and as soon as the women saw my long hair they all began sharpening their scissors. I put my hands over my hair and explained over and over that I didn't want it cut, trimmed, shaped, or touched with scissors. I only wanted it curled up and fixed to make me look different. They reluctantly put away their scissors and began working on it. After three hours of shampoo, curlers, and melting my ears under a dryer, they turned me out of the beauty shop. My hair was piled up so high that I felt as if I had a pumpkin on my head. In addition to my new hairdo, I had a new face; they had put makeup, eye shadow, eye liner, mascara, eyebrow pencil, and lipstick on me. I was convinced that now I looked just like everyone else, and I knew Don would be thrilled with the "new me."

He was not thrilled. He walked through the door, looked at me, and asked, "Did it take long to do that to yourself?"

"It took all day. Do you like the way I look?"

He didn't have to think twice for an answer. "No, I liked you the way you were."

"I wanted to look nice. I wanted to look like everyone else so you wouldn't be ashamed of me."

"I'm never ashamed of you, and one of the reasons I married you was because you *weren't* like everyone else. You were different. I liked you for being different. Don't try to be something you're not. Be yourself."

I felt foolish. I had spent a lot of time and money just to end up looking silly. Tears began to trickle down my face, leaving black streaks of mascara.

Don touched my hair, which was stiff from hair spray.

"Why don't you go see if you can find my wife under there someplace, and if you can, tell her I'll take her out to dinner."

125

I stood in the shower and washed the new me away. A half-hour later I returned to the living room—long dress, no makeup, and hair in braids.

Don gave one of my braids a tug. "Now *that's* my wife!"

I reached up and touched his face. His beard was gone; he had shaved it off.

"Let's go eat," he said and smiled.

To celebrate the old me, Don took me to a seafood restaurant. When I looked at the menu my stomach turned over. I didn't think I could make myself eat anything that didn't walk across the land on four legs or fly on two wings. Something that wiggled through the water just didn't seem fit to eat.

Don ordered salmon steaks and waited for me to order. I asked for a tuna sandwich, which didn't sound as bad as some of the things they offered. When it came to the table, I picked up one half in my hands, prayed I wouldn't get sick, and then felt my throat close up tight. I quickly shoved the sandwich into my coat pocket and waited for my chance to get rid of the other half. As soon as I was sure Don wasn't watching, I shoved the other half of the tuna sandwich into my other coat pocket.

"See, dear, eating fish doesn't hurt you. It's just a case of mind over matter."

Sure, I thought to myself, *if you don't mind squashed tuna sandwiches in your pockets, it doesn't matter.*

On the drive home the car heater was on, and the warm air spread the odor of tuna through the car.

Don kept sniffing the air. "I could swear I smell fish!"

"It must be your imagination," I said and wished he would hurry home.

After we arrived home I hurried into the kitchen and began digging out the tuna and stuffing it into the garbage disposal, trying to get my pockets cleaned out before Don came inside.

126

A few minutes later he came in and found me sitting on the couch and watching TV.

"I'm sorry," he said.

"What for?" I asked.

"For trying to force you to eat fish. There's no reason in the world why you should have to eat fish," he said.

"All right, we'll forget it." I let out a sigh of relief.

"I'll take your coat to the cleaner tomorrow," he offered.

I sank down farther on the couch and kept my eyes on the TV set.

"As long as we're on the subject of food—do you think we could sometimes have a vegetable other than corn?"

"Corn is best. Indians have eaten corn since the beginning."

"I like corn, but we've had it every meal since we've been married. Maybe we could try some different things sometimes."

I nodded. For the next month we had peas at every meal, and following that we went back to corn.

"Honey, these pants are too long. Do you think you could take them up about an inch in the cuff? I'm in sort of a hurry, I wanted to wear them today," Don said.

I took the pants and hurried to the next room. I knew that it would take me a long time to stitch up the cuffs by hand, but I hadn't yet mastered the sewing machine Don had bought me. I decided to compromise. I rolled up the cuffs and grabbed the stapler out of Don's desk and quickly stapled the cuffs into place.

I handed his pants back to him. He looked at them and put them on without saying a word and left.

Later that night I awoke and discovered he was not in bed. I got up and followed the trail of light coming from the bathroom.

He was sitting on the edge of the bathtub sewing on the cuffs of his pants. I sneaked back to bed. I vowed I would not use the stapler anymore.

Chapter Fourteen

"What was Christmas like for you when you were a kid?" Don asked.

"We didn't celebrate Christmas. We didn't believe in God," I answered.

"Lots of people celebrate Christmas who don't believe in God," Don said. "You mean you didn't do anything at all about Christmas?"

"No—oh, I remember once a girl friend of one of my uncles gave me a present. It was a little bottle of hand lotion. I'd never had anything like that before. It seemed like such a grown-up gift, and I was so proud of it, that I decided not to use it so it would last forever."

"Did it last forever?" he asked.

"No. That night I hid it under my bed and it froze. The next morning when I woke up and looked for my wonderful treasure, there was nothing left but broken glass and frozen hand-lotion. I didn't even get to use one drop," I sighed. "What were your Christmases like when you were a little boy?"

"Awful. My folks were too cheap to buy me or my sister any presents. One year I hung up a stocking for Santa Claus to fill. I wanted a baseball more than anything in the world, and when I saw something big and round in the toe of my stocking on Christmas morning, I thought I'd gotten my baseball. But it was an orange. I hate oranges to this day." He was quiet a moment. "If my folks had been too poor to buy gifts, I could have understood. But even if you're poor, you can still make toys for your kids. I was just cheap labor to them. I worked harder than any hired hand ever did on that ranch. I earned my own living from the time I was ten years old, and as soon as I was old enough to drive I saved money to buy an old pickup truck and I ran away from home and headed for Alaska. It was as far away from Texas as I could get."

"What happened to your family?" I asked.

"I guess they are still on the ranch. My sister got married as soon as she could, to get away from home," he said.

"Do you think you'll ever see them again?"

"No. Cry, my folks are—" he sighed. "They are bad medicine. My dad drinks, and my mother is—well, she's real bad. My sister and I got away from them as soon as we could. I think of myself as an orphan because I never had real parents. I wasn't a son, I was free labor. You'd do me a favor by never talking about my childhood or my family again. I'd like to forget everything that ever happened to me before I met you. You're the only good thing that ever happened to me."

It was our first Christmas together, and I wanted it to be special. For the first time in my life I had someone of my very own to give a present to.

I started decorating too early, but I was too excited to wait any longer. Our Christmas tree was up and decorated on the last day of November.

I shopped for hours to find a special gift for my husband, but nothing seemed right, until one day I was looking at men's shirts and I found the answer. I would make him a Cherokee chief shirt! I bought a pale blue shirt and yards of brightly colored ribbon. At home I sewed the ribbons onto the shirt with tiny

130

stitches. I slipped it on and twirled around. The red, yellow, blue, and green ribbons flew out around me in a rainbow of color. He would love it! A chief's shirt! I was sure he had never had one before, and I proudly wrapped it and placed it gently under our tree.

Don placed gifts under the tree, too, and I shook, pinched and squeezed each of them until the Christmas paper was wrinkled and the bows were loose.

He scolded me and threatened to hide them if I didn't leave them alone, but I couldn't walk past the gifts without giving one of them a jab with my finger.

"You should let me open them now. What if something happened and I died before Christmas? I would never know what you gave me!"

But Don would only laugh and add more tape to the gifts.

On Christmas Eve we sat in the dark, watching the lights twinkle on the tree and listening to Christmas carols from the stereo.

In my heart was great loneliness and longing for my friends back home. An occasional tear trickled down my cheeks. When the stereo played "I'll Be Home for Christmas" the trickle turned into a river, and I buried my face in my hands and cried.

Don knew what was wrong without asking and left me alone with my attack of homesickness.

I was just getting down to some real crying when I felt the house tremble. My tears were quickly forgotten and my heart froze.

"What's that!" I whispered.

"It's just a little earth tremor," Don said.

The house shook again and the dishes rattled in the cupboard and a window cracked.

"It's an earthquake!" I shouted. I grabbed one of my presents and leaped into the middle of our bed. "We're going to be killed! I told you something would happen! Give me my presents now!"

The house gave a hard shake and the Christmas tree lights went out. I was left standing in the middle of the bed with a half-opened gift in my hands. There was a deep silence as we waited to see if there were going to be any more tremors or if the ground was going to open up and swallow us alive.

The light flickered back on, and Don switched on a few lamps. He pulled the half-opened gift out of my hands and started to put it back under the tree.

"Good grief! What on earth?" he exclaimed and I followed him over to the tree.

Standing in a pile of pine needles was a scraggly stick with lights and baubles draped on it. I had put the tree up too early, and it had dried out. The earthquake had shaken every needle off the tree. We now had the ugliest Christmas tree in the whole world! Homesickness was forgotten as we burst into laughter.

We decided to open our gifts instead of waiting until morning. Don handed me three packages, and I ripped them open eagerly. Inside the first one was a silver cross on a chain, and I put it around my neck before I opened the other two. The second package held a tiny whale he had carved from wood, and the last gift was a fuzzy pink robe.

"Thank you. They are wonderful gifts!" I said holding the whale he had carved and pulling on the pretty, warm robe. "I like them all very much. Now you must open your gift!" I handed him his present and waited eagerly as he opened it.

"What a nice—" He held it up and let the colored ribbons dangle down the front and back of the shirt. "It's a very nice— What is it?"

"It's a Cherokee chief's shirt!" I said and helped him put it on.

He looked in the mirror. "I'm not a Cherokee chief," he said. "You don't like it, do you?" I was disappointed. "I keep forgetting you aren't an Indian. I should have bought you a present for a white man."

"I like it, really I do. It's just that I've never had a shirt like this before, and I was surprised. It's real nice," he said, and started to take it off. Then he looked at my face and put it back on. "It's such a nice shirt I was going to save it for good, but I like it so much I think I'll wear it right now, for Christmas Eve." He looked at himself in the mirror again.

"I can cut the ribbons off," I offered.

"No, you went to a lot of work to sew them on. You leave it the way it is. I'm probably the only man in Alaska with a chief's shirt. In fact, I'd bet on it." He smiled. "Merry Christmas, Crying Wind. I love you."

"Merry Christmas," I answered. I wondered if I should say "I love you" back to him, but I didn't think I could ever make my tongue say those words as long as I lived.

We took one last look at our pitiful tree and went to bed. Around my neck I wore the silver cross, and I slid the little whale under my pillow.

It was the best Christmas I had ever had.

Chapter Fifteen

We didn't have any close neighbors, and it was hard for me to make new friends, so I clung desperately to my old friends back in Colorado. Writing letters became a part of my daily routine, and I waited anxiously for their answers. A letter from a friend at church made my new life a little less lonely, a little less frightening. I saved every letter I received and read them again on the days I didn't get any mail.

I waited eagerly for the mailman to come each day and was upset if he was late. My days became "good" days if I received a lot of mail and "bad" days if the mailbox was empty.

A LETTER FROM HOME

The mailman has come! I ran through the snow,
My feet were numb, it was twenty below.
A letter from you, though it didn't say much—
Just a line or two to keep in touch.
You spoke of spring and the early flowers.
And how you'd watched the robins for hours and
    hours.
The snow was gone and the grass was green,
You'd been working hard and the house was clean.
Things back home were just the same,
There wasn't much news, but you couldn't complain.

134

A couple of old friends had asked about me
The other day when they stopped by for tea.
Well, you had to close, it was time to go,
But you'd write again in a week or so.
My frozen fingers clutched the letter you wrote,
As I stood by the mailbox without my coat.
But I didn't notice the cold or the storm,
Because for a few minutes I'd been back home, safe
and warm.

But one day I received a letter that broke my heart. It was a cold, bitter January. I was chilled to the bone, and nothing could keep me warm. I wore extra clothes and hovered around the stove trying to keep away the chill. I remembered how freezing cold it had been in the tar-paper house back on the reservation. Sometimes I felt as if I had been cold all my life. How I longed for a blazing yellow sun to burn life back into my shivering body.

It came in the morning mail. A letter from Sally saying Audrey had died. My eyes flooded with tears, and my hands shook so badly I could hardly read the rest of the letter. Audrey and Reverend McPherson had finished dinner and had gone in to watch television. In an instant, she was gone. She had died so peacefully, so quietly, that Reverend McPherson, who was sitting next to her, didn't even know she had been called home. He had asked her a question, and when she didn't answer he looked over at her and thought she had fallen asleep. When he tried to wake her, he found she was dead.

My heart cried out in agony. *Audrey! My friend, gone!* I wept for hours and shivered now from an inner cold that came from losing a friend. Audrey's death left me in a black hole of depression. I missed her terribly and didn't understand why she

135

had to die when she was so good and so many people needed her. I was angry with God for letting someone I loved die. I knew I should be happy for Audrey; she was now standing in the presence of the almighty God, and her joy was full. But I was too grief stricken to feel anything but my own loss.

It wasn't until Reverend McPherson wrote to me that I was able to accept her death as God's perfect will. Through his own grief and loneliness, Reverend McPherson wrote of his great, loving Savior, who had called Audrey home. He knew there would be only a short separation before they would be reunited someday in heaven. His faith took the sting out of death for me and I realized that death is not final for a Christian—it is only a step into eternal life!

Chapter Sixteen

The snow brushed against the windows with a whispering, haunting sound. Don came inside in a flurry of snow, brushing it off his parka and letting it fall to the floor.

"I'll be gone longer this time," he said. He had told me that several times before.

"I know. I'll be all right," I repeated.

He was flying hundreds of miles north, beyond the Arctic Circle, to work on an oil rig.

"I'll be fine. I just wish the sun would come back. It's so hard to live in the darkness." I walked over to the window and looked out into the Alaskan winter night that would last for months. Months of darkness, months of waiting for the sun to come back again.

"What do you see, Crying Wind?" Don asked.

"Nothing," I answered. How could I tell him I saw faraway mountains and dense forests? Indians racing across rolling prairies on wild-eyed ponies under the hot summer sun? How could I tell him I saw herds of thundering buffalo in the clouds? His gray eyes could never see the things my brown eyes saw. His ears would never hear the ancient drums beating in my heart.

He was gone again and it might be weeks before he would

137

return. I curled up in the warm cabin with a dozen books and shut out the world.

Three days later the wind was howling like a hungry wolf and it blew the crystal snow against the windows so hard that it sounded like pebbles hitting the glass. All morning the snow piled higher and by noon I knew there would be no letup. If the storm lasted much longer I would be snowed in, and there wasn't any food left in the cabin. It had been a mistake to let the supplies run so low; now I would have to go out in the storm to get food.

I pulled on my leather jacket and tied a scarf around my head. I stepped outside into a blinding white world. The flakes were falling so fast and thick it was hard to see more than a few feet ahead, and I prayed I would not lose my way.

In spite of the deep snow, it didn't take long to walk the two miles to the trading post. I knew I was buying too many groceries, but I was hungry, and would need food for several days. When I lifted the two large grocery sacks, I staggered under their weight.

Although it wasn't long past noon, it was already growing dark. As I hurried on my way home, the sacks felt heavier with each step. At the end of the first mile I was so overheated and tired that I stopped and set the groceries in the snow. I took off my coat and threw it down and sat on it until I could get my second wind. I cooled off quickly and put my coat back on. Then I picked up the sacks and walked toward home.

I was gasping for breath when I staggered through the cabin door. I dumped the groceries on the table. My lungs ached and my throat felt funny. I tried to put away my supplies, but I was too weak, so I only set the milk and meat outside in the little igloo we had made. Then I heated a can of soup and took a few sips, but my throat was too sore to swallow, so I went to bed.

When I woke up late the next day, I had an uneasy feeling that I had something more serious than a cold. My chest felt as if giant buffalo were standing on my lungs, and I could manage only short, shallow breaths. I lay in bed and watched the snow drift up against the window until it piled higher than the top of the window and I could no longer see out at all.

I was too weak to get out of bed, and sitting up made me dizzy. I was on fire with fever, and each breath I took sounded like a death rattle. I dozed off and on, grateful when I could sleep and be unaware of the pain in my chest.

After midnight the next day the wind stopped blowing as suddenly as if someone had shut a door. The furnace quit, and I was without heat. I tried to pray, but my mind wandered so badly I could say only a few words at a time before I would float back into my past, back to the days when I was a child playing in the warm, yellow sun. I thought of my mother, a small delicate woman with sad eyes. Then my mind would come back to the present.

I felt as if knives were stabbing my lungs, and I coughed blood.

"I'm dying," I said in a voice so hoarse I couldn't believe it was my own. "I'm dying here in a cold, dark place far from home."

Home. Home, where it was warm and where friends smiled at you.

Then, raising myself on my elbow, I cried out a name I hadn't spoken aloud in years. "Mother," I sobbed, "Mother! I want my mother!" Once again I was a tiny child needing comfort, needing help, afraid and cold and hungry and sick. All the years

139

apart didn't matter now; nothing was important. I just wanted her here with me.

I fell back on the bed. "If I live through this, I'm going to find her," I whispered. "I want to see my mother."

Some machinery broke down and they sent the men home a week early. When Don arrived he found me huddled in bed under coats and blankets. I was shivering and spitting blood.

He took me to the clinic, and I could hear a doctor talking to Don.

"She would do better in a warm, dry climate. Like so many Indians, she has weak lungs caused from cold, drafty houses and a poor diet when she was young. She's lucky you came home when you did."

I closed my eyes and thanked God for sparing my life. I was sure it was no accident that the oil rig had broken down and that Don had come home early.

I recovered in a few days, but I had a racking cough that lasted for months.

When I was feeling better, Don took me on a tour of Alaska. We visited tiny trading posts along our way and watched herds of caribou migrating and the great, ugly moose feeding in the marshy valleys. Of all the places we visited, I liked Homer best. The docks, with dozens of fishing boats, looked like pictures in a book. Don showed me one boat that he had worked on when he was fishing for king crab. I made sketches and wrote poetry along the way, and we spent hours beachcombing and watching the waves roll in. I was struck with the vastness of the great water, the Pacific Ocean.

"Crying Wind has seen the Pacific Ocean!" I yelled, and splashed in the icy water.

"And the Pacific Ocean has seen Crying Wind!" Don yelled.

140

"It's not impressed!" I laughed.
Those days of freedom and rest did a lot to restore my health,
and I was feeling much stronger when we returned to our cabin.

HOMESICK

The aching loneliness I feel inside,
For those of you who live "outside,"
Can't be hidden under a blanket of white,
Nor swept away by the northern lights.

The mountains, glorious though they may be,
Are only a barrier between you and me;
I remain a captive in this frozen land,
Held here by the icy grip of its hand.

In summer warmth the forget-me-not grows,
And quickly dies as the autumn wind blows,
And my lonely heartache starts anew,
Another long winter here—without you.

THE WEATHERMAN

"Oh, the winters aren't so bad here,
It only lasts ten months they say;
We had a dandy summer last year,
I think it was on a Thursday."
"Yeah, that's right because Friday was fall.
Can't complain though,
Some years we don't have any summer at all!"

THE ICE WORM TURNETH

Alaska, your heart is frozen,
You have no compassion for man;

141

You hide behind ice and eternal cold
As you jealously hoard your land.

You're the Great Land!
The land of moose and beaver,
The land of whales and caribou,
The land of cabin fever.

You are an unforgiving land,
But, Oh! Would I leave you if I could?
You bet your sweet life I would!

TOTEM POLE

A blind old totem stood alone,
And quaked with inward fear,
Afraid of being all alone,
Never seeing other totems near.
His eyes stared only straight ahead,
He forgot his friends nearby.
He flung out his arms in hopelessness
And uttered forlorn cries.
His tears ran streaming down his cheeks,
The years passed swiftly on,
The rain and snow took their toll,
Leaving his face sad and long.
He was never alone, because close at hand,
Others like him stood;
But he never knew, because just like them,
His eyes were carved from wood.
Many times we don't see friends,
As close by as they may be;
Perhaps we are just as blind
As the totem who could not see.

Chapter Seventeen

Don had a high school education, but he could hardly read or write. When he read, it took him a long time to struggle through a simple paragraph, and when he wrote, his handwriting and spelling were so bad they were nearly impossible to make out.

"I don't understand how you can have so little education and can read and write so well, and I wasted twelve years in school and almost have to sign my name with an X!" Don laughed.

"Grandmother taught me to read paperback novels when I was five years old. I was raised on western novels and Agatha Christie murder mysteries. By the time I was eight years old I knew fifty ways to poison someone. I've read at least three books a week for years—that makes a lot of reading. Maybe public education is a handicap," I said.

"Would you like to go back to school and get a diploma?" Don asked while he stacked up my latest pile of books.

My heart froze and I felt sick. I sank down into a chair.

"Go back to school?" Into my mind came pictures of people throwing rocks and teachers laughing at me. "No! I would never go back to school!"

Don went on, "I saw an advertisement today saying that the university is offering correspondence courses in several different subjects. I thought you might like to take one."

"You are ashamed of me because I'm uneducated!" I accused.

"No, that's not true. I just think you can be more than you are, that's all. You have a good mind. You read more books in a week than I'll read in my lifetime. I just thought you might like to study and learn more." He tossed a booklet on the table. "Look at this, then decide, OK?"

I picked up the booklet and flipped through it. There were twenty-five courses offered. I didn't even know what most of them were about, but one was called "Indian Anthropology." That might be interesting; it was a course on ancient American Indians. I read it aloud to Don.

"That's just right for you. Why don't you sign up for it?" He was enthusiastic.

"All right." I sulked as I filled out the form for the university. If he wanted a high school graduate for a wife, he should have married one!

In a week some books came in the mail and were soon followed by my first lesson. I was back in school again, the thing I hated the most in my life. It was a correspondence course, but it was still connected with school.

I enjoyed reading the books, and the questions on the lessons weren't as hard as I had expected them to be. The books said that people started out as slimy cells in the ocean, and in a few million years they became apes. Then they lost their hair, turned different colors, and became men. The course was supposed to take a year, but I had a lot of spare time and I finished it in six months. When I received an *A* for the course, Don was beside himself with excitement.

"You did great! I knew you could do it! You could probably get some kind of a degree if you worked at it. What do you think you'll take next?" He took a thumbtack and stuck my grade paper to the wall.

"Take next? You didn't tell me I had to take more courses!

144

I thought if I did good on this I could quit! I don't want to go to school! Why are these papers so important?" I reached up and jerked the grade paper off the wall, threw it on the floor, and ran into the bedroom, slamming the door behind me.

Don followed me in a few seconds holding the paper in his hand.

"I'm sorry. I thought you would enjoy studying, since you read all the time anyway. I thought you would like to set a goal for yourself. I thought I was helping you. You don't ever have to take any school courses again," he said.

I stopped crying. "I like reading and learning things, but I don't need a piece of paper from somebody telling me what I've learned. That piece of paper doesn't make me any smarter."

I was angry with Don. Because of him I had a government Social Security number and a driver's license. And now I had taken a course from some school to learn about Indians, and they thought Indians came from a cell in the ocean and weren't even created by God!

Like most white people, Don thought what was written on a piece of paper was important. Like most Indians, I didn't think anything written on a piece of paper was important.

Weeks went by. The conscious and unconscious hurts and slights made me depressed and weary. I decided I had had enough of this married life. I would divorce Don and return south, where the sun was warm and where I wouldn't be up to my neck in papers. Mr. Stafford could stay here with his papers and his snow! I'd show him!

I ran to the closet and took out all his clothes and laid them in a pile. Next I emptied his drawers and folded everything neatly. Then I pulled the blanket off our bed and cut it in half and wrapped his clothing in his half of the blanket. I carried it

145

outside and set it in front of the door. Last I placed his shoes beside the blanket, with the toes pointing away from the door.

I stood back and looked at it. There! Now we were divorced, Indian style!

I went back inside and shut the door. I would never see him again.

I sat down and began painting on some rabbit skins. At exactly five-thirty, the front door opened, and in walked Don holding his blanket and clothes under one arm and his shoes in his hand.

I stood up. "What are you doing here?" Didn't he know I had divorced him? When a man saw his belongings outside the door, with his shoes pointing away, he picked up his things and left. He didn't come barging back inside with his clothes bundled under his arm!

"Is this dry cleaning, or were you just cleaning out closets?" he asked and dropped everything onto the couch. He held up his half of the torn blanket. "What happened to this?" he asked.

I stood there with my hands on my hips. Didn't he know anything? I looked at him a minute, then decided I might as well let it drop for the time being. I walked over and grabbed the blanket out of his hands and headed toward the bedroom.

"What are you going to do?" he asked.

"I'm going to sew our blanket back together," I said, and wondered how he had survived this long when he didn't know anything. I would have to find another way to end this marriage; Don didn't know how to play by Indian rules.

Don told me every day that he loved me, but I had learned at a very early age never to trust anyone, so I didn't believe him. I was sure it was just something he said because he felt he was

146

supposed to. After all, what did it cost him? They were only words; words are cheap. Still, I could never bring myself to say "I love you" to him.

I kept remembering what Flint had said the last time I had seen him. "What could he possibly see in you? Why would any man want to marry you?" I couldn't think of a single reason why Don should want me. He could have married prettier girls, girls who would say "I love you" and mean it. He must realize by now that he had made a terrible mistake, and soon he would leave me and never come back. What would become of me when he left? I didn't know anyone up here; I was far from my home. He would probably throw me out with only the clothes on my back, and I would freeze or starve.

I decided that since it was only a matter of time before he would walk out on me, I would walk out on him first. People had run out on me all my life; I was always ending up broke, scared and alone. But this time I would be smart—this time I would do the leaving!

I knew that I had made vows in church and before God to love, honor, and obey this man until I died, so I was very careful not to ask God's opinion of my idea. I knew He wouldn't approve. I would go ahead and leave, and when I got safely back home I would ask God to forgive me and hope he wouldn't strike me dead with a bolt of lightning.

I began to make my plans. I saved the money I made from my paintings and planned to leave in a few weeks. I didn't mention it to Don; it was my secret. Don had been kind to me, and I was grateful for that, but I was sure things were near the end for us, and I was restless. I was very careful not to do anything that would cause Don to suspect what I was going to do. I was sure he didn't know a thing.

147

A week before I planned to leave, Don brought home a shoe box and handed it to me. When I opened it, I found a darling, black, fuzzy kitten inside.

"He's beautiful! Where did you get him?" I asked.

"There was an ad in the newspaper," he said and petted the kitten.

I held the ball of soft fur against my cheek. "What's its name?"

"Stay Awhile," he answered.

I looked up into Don's gray eyes, and they seemed to bore into my mind and read my thoughts.

"What?"

"His name is Stay Awhile," he said. "I'll go get him some milk." And he disappeared into the kitchen.

I held the cat on my lap. Did Don know? He couldn't! I had been too careful. It was a coincidence.

"Stay Awhile," I repeated, when Don came back. "That's no name for a cat."

"I thought it was a good name. Maybe it will keep him from running away and getting lost." Don scratched the kitten behind its ear and it purred loudly and lapped up some milk from the saucer.

The kitten soon took over our cabin and seemed to think he owned it and we were his pets. I was determined not to become attached to him because I knew I would be leaving soon. I had already packed my suitcase with a few clothes and had slid it under the bed to hide it from Don. I would only take what I had had before we were married, and that wasn't much; it easily fit into one suitcase.

The time came for me to leave. I had avoided looking into Don's eyes all day, afraid he would be able to see what I was thinking. I wasn't sure what he would do if he knew I was going to leave him that night. I kept myself busy cleaning the house and cooking. I had baked two apple pies so he would have something to eat after I left. I tried not to think about what I was doing, because if I did, I became confused and I knew it was really a very simple thing: I was just leaving Don before he left me.

When I was sure Don was asleep, I quietly slipped out of bed and tiptoed into the bathroom, where I quickly dressed and gathered up a few last-minute things to put into my suitcase. In an hour I would be on an airplane headed back home. Nothing could stop me from leaving now.

I carefully pulled the suitcase out from under the bed, praying I wouldn't wake up Don. I opened it to put the last of my things inside and found a piece of paper lying on top of my clothing. I picked up the scrap of paper, and in the dim light I read, "I Love You. Please Don't Go."

Don knew! He had known all along!

I stood there in the darkness, with tears streaming silently down my face. Stay Awhile stretched, rolled over in his box, and went back to sleep.

If I didn't leave soon I would miss my plane. If I stayed, what would happen to me? What if Don left me and I was all alone again?

Then I could hear God's voice in my heart. *Don isn't the one standing here with a suitcase and sneaking off in the middle of the night like a thief! Don is asleep in his bed, where he is supposed to be. He's not going anywhere! You asked me to give you a husband, and I did. Don't you think I knew who was the right one for you?*

I closed the suitcase quietly and slid it back under the bed. I slipped out of my clothes and climbed carefully into bed so I wouldn't wake up Don. Maybe I really could trust him; maybe he really did love me and wouldn't leave me.

"All right, God," I prayed, "I'll stay."

I fell asleep holding the note tightly in my hand—a note written in pencil on a scrap of paper; a note that said, "I Love You. Please Don't Go."

Chapter Eighteen

Neither of us ever mentioned the note in the suitcase. We both pretended nothing had ever happened.

I decided that I didn't love Don, but I could pretend I did. And if I pretended well enough, he would never know the difference.

I began trying out recipes in the cookbook Don bought me, and I learned to sew his clothes on the sewing machine instead of stapling them. I tried to keep my fire-red temper under control and to keep our home peaceful and comfortable. I would ask myself, *What would I do for Don today if I really loved him?* and I would polish his boots or bake a pie. I knew I was doing a good job of fooling him, because he seemed much happier than he had before.

Summer came, and the sun made up for not shining all winter. I loved the long days and didn't go to bed until three o'clock in the morning because it was still light out. Don took me for long drives in the wild countryside, and we went camping and hiking and paddled a canoe up icy rivers. It felt good to be close to mother earth again and to feel the wind and sun and to walk through tall grass and giant trees.

One day we walked for miles through a dense forest where ferns were taller than we were. We picked berries and dug up

151

fossils. It was a beautiful day, and we were so far out in the wilderness I felt we were the only two people in the world.

When we stopped for a rest Don reached down and picked up a dandelion and handed it to me. "Have a sunshine flower," he said.

Suddenly the memories of the day he had "come courting" with penny suckers and dandelions flooded back. We had been married nearly a year now, and he had brought me more happiness than I had ever dreamed possible.

"I love you," I said. My words hung in the air like a bird in mid-flight. I couldn't believe I had said them, and Don couldn't believe he had heard them. I didn't know which of us was more surprised.

"I love you," I repeated and found it easier to say the second time. "I really do!" And my heart burst with feelings I had kept buried all my life. I flung myself into Don's arms, overcome with the joy of falling in love with my husband.

Our love grew, and each day was an adventure. Two lonely people would never be lonely again. When he was away working in the oil fields, we wrote to each other every day, and when he was home it was a celebration.

As women have from the beginning of time, I began to pray I could give a child, the greatest gift of all, to the man I loved.

Countless times I would pray, "Lord, please give us a son, and I will raise him up to worship you."

When time passed and there was no child, I began to fear I would remain barren. I would become a dry, twisted, old oak that had never borne fruit. I sat in the darkness many nights and wept bitter tears. I had been cheated many times in life, but this time Don was being cheated, too, and that made the emptiness hurt more.

I tried to pray "Thy will be done" and accept that there would

152

My Son —
Know the
Earth

always be just the two of us. We loved each other and had more happiness than most people. I should have been satisfied, but I wasn't.

I began to grow angry. I felt God had turned against me. Other women had children—why not me? Animals had off-spring—why not me?

"No, God! I can't pray 'Thy will be done' if it's Your will for me to be childless! I won't give up. I'll beg You for a child a hundred times a day every day for the rest of my life! I want a child! Give me a son, and I promise I'll raise him to worship You." Hundreds of times my lips uttered that prayer, "Give me a son! Give me a son!"

I searched the Bible, reading every passage that mentioned children, and I soon found out that in ancient times it was a disgrace for a woman to be childless.

Rachel was barren and then "she conceived, and bare a son; and said, God hath taken away my reproach," in the book of Genesis.

In the book of 1 Samuel, Hannah wept and prayed to the Lord, "If thou . . . wilt give unto thy handmaid a man child, then I will give him unto the LORD."

"Children are an heritage of the LORD: and the fruit of the womb is his reward," wrote the psalmist. If children were a reward, then I would remain childless, because I had done nothing to deserve a reward from God.

But I clung to the Bible stories of women who had been barren and then later had children. They were my hope, and I suffered with Rachel and Hannah and rejoiced because their prayers were answered.

I bought infant clothes and blankets and rattles and hid them away where Don couldn't see them. He wouldn't understand; he would think I was losing my mind.

154

On days when I was depressed, I would get out the baby clothes and hold them against my heart and would close my eyes and again say, "Please, God, give me a son."

One September night, as the moon hung just above the tree-tops and the wind tore the leaves off the limbs, leaving them naked and cold, I stood at the window and for the thousandth time made my plea to God. "Give me a son, and I'll raise him to glorify you."

The scene before me disappeared, and instead of the moon I saw a huge eagle flying across the sky. Instead of trees I saw a high, rugged cliff with a nest tucked in a crevice. The eagle landed on her nest and folded her wings and settled herself on several eggs. An instant later, the eagle spread her wings and fled down the canyon. She was followed by baby eagles.

The vision disappeared. Once again the moon and the trees were before me. I rubbed my eyes and looked again. The night was the same. There had been no eagle, no cliff, no eggs; but I had seen them as clearly as anything I had ever seen in bright daylight.

"Thank You, God. I know that was Your answer. I know that at this very minute I carry my son beneath my heart." And I wept for joy.

I started to wake up Don to tell him, but I was afraid he wouldn't believe me. He would say I had imagined it or dreamed it. There was no way I could put the beauty of the vision into words. It was too special, too precious, a secret between God and myself.

I was like Rachel; God had taken away my reproach. He had answered my prayer.

I made a pair of tiny baby moccasins out of the softest leather I could find and sewed blue beads on them.

I stood before my husband and handed him my gift. "These are for your son," I said, trying hard not to show the great excitement and pride in my pounding heart.

"My son?" he smiled. He could see the light in my face, and he knew God had blessed us. "Maybe it will be a girl," he said, looking at the blue beads.

"No," I answered, "a man must have a son. I asked for a son. That's what it will be."

I counted the days with great happiness and spent my time making things for our baby and praying for his safe journey into our world.

I took a branch from a willow and bent it into a small hoop and took long grass and weaved it back and forth, leaving only one tiny hole in the center. I hung it above the bed we had for our baby. It was a dream net like those Indian mothers had made for their babies since the beginning of time. The net would catch and hold all the bad dreams, and only good, sweet dreams could get through the tiny hole in the center. My baby would sleep in happiness. I made a wooden cradleboard to carry my baby, and more clothes than he could ever wear.

It was a happy time for me, and Don was even more thoughtful than he had been before.

I sometimes found myself wondering what I would have done if he had left me, as Flint had said he would. Would I have been so eager to have this child? What if I had had a child and been alone, as my mother had been? For the first time I had an inkling of her side of the story. She had been married too young to a man who didn't love her. When he had walked out on her, she must have been frightened and terribly hurt. It was easier now to understand why she had left me with Grandmother. I wished she knew she was going to be a grandmother now.

Don urged me to go to a doctor. But Grandmother had had

eleven children at home—surely I could have one at home. The idea of going to a hospital terrified me. I had heard terrible stories about hospitals. I had heard they cut off all your hair and shaved your head. They kept you there as long as they wanted to and you couldn't get out. And sometimes they made mistakes and operated on the wrong people. I didn't want to go to a hospital. I wasn't sick; I was only having a baby.

On a Monday morning I knew it was time for the baby to come. My heart beat fast as I realized that in a few hours I would be a mother. When Don came home from work that night I told him it wouldn't be long; the time for the baby to arrive was near.

Hours passed and the pains grew worse. Night passed and morning came. Don stayed beside my bed. Neither of us slept all night, and my strength was gone.

"It's taking too long," Don said. "I'm taking you to the hospital."

I began to cry, "No! Wait! He'll come when he's ready." And I begged him not to take me to the hospital.

A nurse at the hospital helped me into a bed. "How long has she been in labor?" she asked.

"About forty hours," Don said in a voice that didn't sound like his at all.

The nurse led Don out of the room, and I cried harder. I wanted to have my baby at home with my husband. Now they had taken him away, and I was alone.

A Kickapoo woman who died in childbirth was considered as having died in battle and was given full honors of a warrior's burial, but that was small comfort now.

Another nurse came in and gave me ice to hold in my mouth. "Don't be afraid," she said and held my hand.

I was sure God had sent an angel to comfort me.

Early Wednesday morning our son was born, a healthy, screaming baby.

"Thank you, God, for our son!" I laughed, "He looks like a baby antelope!" And that's how he was named—our firstborn son, Little Antelope.

Don was standing against the doors of the delivery room so that when the nurse flung the doors open to wheel out my bed, they hit him in the back.

"We've got a son!" I laughed, "We've got a son!"

Later, when I held Little Antelope for the first time, tears ran down my cheeks. How beautiful, how precious he was! My son! I was a mother; I had been blessed by God to bring life into the world. Never again would I feel useless or ugly. I had borne a son!

When it came time to fill out the birth certificate, Don insisted we give the baby a Christian name as well as Little Antelope, so our son became Aaron Little Antelope Stafford.

Back home again, I stood beside our baby's crib for hours, amazed at the miracle of life. At night I would creep into his room to make sure he was still there and still breathing. "Don and me and baby makes three," I would whisper.

When I heard the hymn "How Great Thou Art," it touched me in a new way. I had always loved hearing about wandering through the forest glades and about the thunder and the stars— these were things I understood. It was a beautiful song. Now when I heard the part that said, "God, His only Son not sparing," tears would rush to my eyes and I would look down at the baby wrapped in the soft blue blanket in my arms. My son! I would never sacrifice my son—no, not even to save every single person in the whole world! And yet God had sacrificed His only Son for people as unworthy as myself. How much more

God loved His Son than I loved mine, and yet how much He loved us to let His Son die so that we could go to heaven! God's sacrifice took on a new and deeper meaning, and I knew I would never take it for granted again. I understood for the first time how much God loved me and what His love had cost Him.

When Little Antelope was seven days old I began reading the Bible to him. God had answered my prayer; now I would keep my promise. Not one day would pass without Little Antelope's hearing God's Word. I figured that if I read a little of the Bible to him each day, I could read it through ten times before he grew up and left home. I wanted him to have God's Word hidden in his heart before he became a man and went out into the world.

When Little Antelope was ten days old, I took him into the woods and removed his blanket and all his clothing and held him up to the sun. "Sun, warm this baby and shine on him always." Then I kneeled down and laid my naked baby on the ground. "My son, meet your grandmother, the earth."

Little Antelope kicked his tiny feet but didn't cry.

> Small baby, naked on the soft floor of the forest,
> Do you hear the heartbeat of your grandmother, the
>   earth?
> Grow, my son, and become strong.
> Be a happy child; be happy as a man.
> Grow my son, strong and wise,
> Do not forget your grandmother, the earth;
> Do not forget your mother in her old age.
> Grow, my son, but not too soon.

"Oh, God, hear me and see the beautiful child You have given me! I dedicated him to You while he kicked beneath my heart.

Every day he will hear of Your love and mercy and greatness!
Let me keep him and raise him for You, and let him grow into
a man and hold his own son in his arms someday. Amen."

I dressed him and wrapped him in his blanket and tied him
back onto his cradleboard and returned to the cabin.

The whole world was beautiful. The future was full of promise. God answers prayer!

Little boy laughing in my arms,
Captured my heart with his little boy charms—
Little boy making my life worth living,
Little boy sharing and loving and giving,
Little boy showing me the world with bright shiny
   eyes,
Putting the sun back into dark, stormy skies.

THE WORLD ON A SILVER PLATTER

I'll give you the world, my son, the world and even
   more;
I'll give you crime and pollution and poverty and war.

Just look at the beautiful cities, my son, the buildings
   are so high;
It's too bad the smog's so thick that you can't see the
   sky.

And see the superhighways, my son, going everywhere,
And see the powerful cars polluting our clean air.

Oh, the wonderful world of science, my son, we've
   made it to the moon;

161

No, I don't think it's true that we'll all be blown up
soon.

Isn't medicine amazing, my son? Now we can nearly
cure cancer.
I wouldn't worry about famines; someone will find an
answer.

Your father and I aren't rich, my son, but we'll give
you your heart's desire;
It's the American way to "charge it" as the cost of living goes higher.

All the finest education, my son—learn to read and
write.
Equal opportunity—it's too bad you're half red and
half white.

You'll have a war of your own; each generation must
have one.
Don't use alcohol or drugs; ignore those who say
they're fun.

It's too bad there's no wilderness left, no wild animals
around,
But we've killed all the animals and subdivided the
ground.

Oh, it's a wonderful world, and I'll give it to you, my
son,
And ask but one small thing in return—forgive us for
what we've done!

YOUR FIRST CHRISTMAS

Sleep warm, my little baby boy;
Beside you is your favorite toy.
It's your first Christmas Eve tonight;
The gifts are wrapped and the tree shines bright.
Here are the gifts I give to you—
A heart full of hope all wrapped in blue.
I'd buy you peace if it could be sold,
And mark it "Fragile" and wrap it in gold.
And I'll tell you a story so you will know,
About a Baby born long ago;
It was the Son of God, who came from above,
And brought us all the Gift of Love.

Chapter Nineteen

Not one child. One is a lonely number. No, there must be at least two. Two to play games—one to chase and one to run.

I didn't know any games, because as a child I had never played. Only once had some children asked me to play hide and seek with them. I had hidden behind some bushes and waited and waited, pleased with myself because I had found such a good hiding place that no one could find me. Then it had slowly dawned on me that no one was looking for me—they had only wanted to get rid of me. "I will never play stupid games again!" I had cried, and I never did.

The "games" my uncles and I had played were not for children. Our games had been shooting tin cans off of each other's heads, shooting at each other's feet to see who would jump first. Savage games, deadly games; racing horses at killing speeds and taking hard falls and rolling in the dust but somehow surviving. No, these were not games for my children. I would buy books. I would learn how to play games, how to be a child again.

When Little Antelope was six months old I found I was going to have another baby.

"I'm sorry, Little Antelope," I whispered to him. "You won't get to be the baby very long."

Don announced he had just lost his job. The company had

closed down, and it didn't look as if he could get another job very soon.

"I think we should leave Alaska. I've heard farms are cheap in Oklahoma. What do you think?" he asked.

"It's warm in Oklahoma! The children can play in the sun! We can have a garden. There are more Indians in Oklahoma than any other state!" I was ready to go.

Don bought a camper, and a week later we started a journey that would take six months. Don wanted to show me as much of the country as he could, so we didn't drive straight to Oklahoma but wandered leisurely through all of the western states. I was sure I would have our second child beside the road in the middle of the Arizona desert, but we finally arrived in Oklahoma, bought a forty-acre farm, and almost had our things unpacked before he was born.

Don took me to an Indian hospital, and our second son came into the world weighing ten pounds and measuring twenty-three inches. He was the largest baby ever born in that hospital. Just before we had left for the hospital, a doe had wandered through our front yard and had walked up to our porch, so we named our new son Lost Deer. Once again Don insisted on a Christian name, and he added Shane to the birth certificate.

Now I had two beautiful sons, and I learned to trust God in a way I never had before.

Six months later I was once again expecting a child. Don shook his head and said, "Don't you think you can stop praying for children now? God has just about blessed us into poverty!"

Now I had two tiny babies to care for, and a third was on the way.

Our farmhouse was old, and the walls had cracks big enough to let "creatures" inside. I killed tarantulas and scorpions and mice and a thousand bugs without names. One day I opened the knife-and-fork drawer and found a snake curled up inside! I slammed the drawer shut so fast it crushed and killed the snake, but for months I couldn't open a drawer without cringing. We covered the house with tar paper in the hopes of keeping the bugs out, but it wasn't long before the strong winds blew all the paper off.

I planted a garden and sang a little song, "Little pregnant mother seeds, will you deliver your children for us?" Most of them didn't deliver, because, unknown to me at the time, Lost Deer had followed along the rows behind me and picked up the seeds I had "spilled" and put them safely into his pocket.

Our only near neighbor was a Cherokee medicine woman. She treated twenty or thirty Indians a week for every sort of ailment, real or imagined. She kept a frog and a hawk in her house for "good medicine" and wore a necklace of eagle claws and one of human bones.

She was called Herb Woman of the Turtle Clan, and there wasn't a plant in the forest she couldn't use for some purpose.

She was wise enough to stay abreast of modern times while keeping one foot in the past. She not only used ancient chants and spells but she also studied astrology and made charts for people according to their stars and Zodiac sign.

One day she asked me what sign I was born under.

"The sign of the cross," I answered.

"There is no sign like that to be born under." She frowned.

"Yes, I was born under the sign of the cross of Calvary," I responded, smiling.

"You're an Indian girl. You best stick to things you know about!" And she went on to tell me stories and legends and the power of "white," or "good," witchcraft. Because she used witchcraft she was called Powacca, meaning "two hearted."

166

So began a friendly battle. She tried to win me back to the "Old Way" and I tried to win her for Christ.

As I was pulling weeds in my garden one day, I found a copperhead snake coiled around a corn stalk just inches from my hand. Cold fear sent me running to the house, and I came back with a gun and shot the head off the snake. Before I left the garden I had killed two more copperheads. As I walked back to the house on weak, trembling legs I praised God for letting me see the snakes before they saw me.

Later, when I told the medicine woman about the copperheads, she scolded me for killing snakes. "All creatures are your brothers. You should not kill except for food! I live here beside a rocky cliff. I see snakes all the time, but I say to them, 'Hello, my brother, let me go in peace!' and the snake god promised he would never harm me."

Walking home from her house I saw a black snake beside our chicken coop.

"Hello, my brother," I said. "Prepare to die!" And I shot him and then looked over my shoulder to see if Herb Woman had been watching.

We had many visits. When she spoke of astrology, I spoke of Jesus. Neither of us ever gave an inch, but we enjoyed each other's company. She was a very special person.

On a rainy day in spring, Herb Woman was found lying dead among astrology charts, packages of herbs, and ceremonial objects in her home. She had died from a snake bite that she had tried to treat herself.

How I hate it when ignorant people say, "The Indian religion is beautiful—let's leave them alone to worship their own gods!" How I wish they could have known and loved Herb Woman and known the terrible loss of her senseless, painful death.

The snake god had failed Herb Woman.

167

Herb Woman of Turtle Clan

Chapter Twenty

Finally all the weariness caught up with me.

"Lord, I'm so tired," I whispered. "Give me strength to get through this day." I pushed up out of bed and stood on shaky legs.

"Lord, I can't make it. I'm too tired." I fell back across the bed. If I could only sleep a few more minutes—even one more minute. "Please, please let me rest!" I begged, but before I had finished my prayer I could hear "Mommy!" coming from the next room.

Tears trickled out of my eyes and slid down my cheeks. I was so tired my body felt like lead. I moved slowly and with great effort.

The night before I had been up sixteen times with the boys. They had earaches and had hardly slept because of the pain. Today they were better, but my head throbbed and my body ached.

Somehow I made it through the morning and praised God when it was time for the children's naps. Now I could lie down and catch up on the sleep I had lost the night before.

On my way to my bedroom the world went black! I rubbed my eyes, but I couldn't see. It was as if a blanket had been thrown over my head. I felt my way to my bed and lay down. I closed my eyes.

169

I'm only tired. I'm only tired. After I rest I'll be fine, I thought.

The children were as tired as I was, and we were all still asleep when Don came home from work. He woke me up, and when I opened my eyes he looked as if he were at the far end of a tunnel, with darkness all around him.

"My eyes are bothering me," I said and rubbed them again. "I can't see right today. I think if I could just sleep awhile I would be all right."

Don looked at my eyes. "I don't see anything wrong with them." He held my hand and noticed my wedding ring was gone. "Where's your ring?"

"It kept falling off, so I put it away," I said.

He dug in the closet until he found the scale and set it beside the bed. "Get on," he ordered.

I stood on the scale while he read the weight. "Ninety-two pounds! You only weigh ninety-two pounds! Where did the other fifteen pounds go? You're pregnant—you should be gaining weight, not losing weight! You lost fifteen pounds!"

I began to cry. Something was wrong! I had lost weight, I couldn't see, and I was so tired I wanted to die.

Early the next morning Don drove me to the doctor for tests. The results of the tests were not good. Four organs were not functioning properly, I had anemia, I was near exhaustion, and my blood cells were malformed and were not producing as they should. In spite of all this, however, the baby seemed to be all right.

The doctor didn't know what was wrong, and some of the tests seemed to contradict each other. All he knew for certain was that my body was not working as it should, and it was affecting my blood.

There were more tests, diets, and medication, but nothing

helped. I was six-months pregnant and still weighed less than a hundred pounds. I looked like a skeleton and had deep, black circles under my eyes. I prayed constantly for my baby to be born normal and healthy.

One doctor suggested I "terminate" my pregnancy, and calling him a murderer, I ran out of his office and refused to go back to him.

Another doctor said I had some of the symptoms of leukemia, but the results of the tests didn't confirm it. I was going into the clinic for blood tests every five days. The doctor talked of starting blood transfusions, but I refused because I was afraid it would do something to my baby.

At home Don took over more and more of the cooking and cleaning. I did as much as I could for the boys, but many days all I could do was sit and hold them in my lap and tell them stories. My vision was so bad it was difficult to read anything. Some days I had double vision, and other days everything looked so dark I would turn on all the lights, hoping they would help me see.

I was so weak I was sure I was dying and couldn't hang on much longer. I had been to so many doctors I couldn't even remember their names, and all they could say was there was something wrong with my blood. They didn't know what it was or what was causing it, but they all agreed it was becoming serious.

I cried. I prayed. I went to more doctors and attended healing services at different churches, all to no avail. Nothing changed the downhill road I was traveling.

I went to a lawyer and made out a will so Don wouldn't have any legal problems after I died. I left instructions that my favorite hymns and Scripture verses be used at my funeral. I was putting my house in order the best way I knew how, and all the time I was asking God, *What will happen to my children?*

171

I wrote long letters to Little Antelope and Lost Deer and put them in their baby books. Above all else, they must know that I loved them with all my heart and that I didn't want to leave them. I told them to obey their father and to follow Jesus. It was hard to put a whole life of teaching into a few pages of a letter.

I told Don he should get married again as soon as he could find a Christian woman who would love him and the children. But I warned over and over that she must be a Christian.

I had worried so much about losing my children that it had never occurred to me that I might die before they did. Now it looked as if my time was running out.

I grieved for all the times I wouldn't be beside their beds to tell them a story and hear their prayers and tuck them in. I felt sorry for all the times they would be sick and have no mother to comfort them. I thought of all the games we would never play, all the walks through an autumn forest we would never take, and all the Christmases we would never celebrate together. It was more than I could bear. I wasn't afraid to die, because I knew that as soon as I had accepted Christ as my Savior I had been given eternal life; when I died I would go to heaven and be with Jesus forever. But I ached for my children, my little orphans. And what about the baby I carried? Would I live long enough to give it life, or would it die with me?

God, let me live long enough to raise my children! Just let me stay here long enough to help them grow up! It was an impossible prayer. With such young children, I would have to live another twenty years to raise them and send them off from home. I was asking God for twenty years, and the doctors couldn't guarantee I would live long enough to have my baby.

Don moved through the house like an old man. He was quiet and he no longer stood tall and proud. His eyes were hollow and sad and he didn't smile anymore.

172

I tried to be brave, but many nights I cried myself to sleep in his arms.

I remembered the lonely days before I had met Don. I recalled how I had tried to kill myself because life hadn't been worth living. Now life was sweet and full. Now that I wanted to live, I was going to die.

I began keeping a diary so there would be something of me left behind for the children. They must remember that I loved them!

THE DIARY

I began this diary to tell you
All of my secrets and dreams,
So I could share a bit of my life—
Oh, how important that seems!

I promise I will write in it
Each day so faithfully;
Perhaps it will help to keep
My life from slipping away from me.

I save pieces of my days
With just a word or two,
And page after page fills up so fast
As I try to say that I loved you.

I take the little book
And put it on the shelf;
I touch it gently and with pride;
The book is part of myself.

If this book is ever read,
Long after I have gone to rest,
Please read the words with love,
And understand I did my best.

Maybe by reading my secret thoughts
You'll know me as no other;
This is the "real me," the inside of the book;
The "me" people saw was only the cover.

So I leave you this book, my children,
Something for you to share,
To tell you how much I love you
And how sorry I am I can't be there.

The days go by as the pages turn,
And someday I know I will find
My name written in God's book of Life,
And I'll go home and leave my diary behind.

Friends everywhere were praying for me. I continued to have blood tests every five days. I did everything the doctors suggested unless there was even the smallest chance of hurting the baby. I would not sacrifice my baby so that I could live.

In the ninth month I gained some weight, and there was more hope for the baby now. Then my right leg became paralyzed, and I had to use crutches to get around.

When at last the time came to go to the hospital, I was sure I would never see my family again. God had let me live long enough to see my baby born. Now my time was at hand.

Trinity Snow Cloud, our third son, was born on a Sunday in January. How we rejoiced that he was healthy and normal, even though he weighed only six pounds.

Within minutes after his birth I noticed there was feeling in my leg again and there was no more pain in my back. I was starving, and a half-hour after the baby was born I was eating supper. I ate continually during the next few days while I rested in the hospital. My vision was normal and I couldn't remember ever feeling so strong.

The doctor said I was better, but he wouldn't say I was well until he took tests.

After I left the hospital I couldn't get enough to eat. I ate as many as six meals a day during the next two weeks. A month later I returned to the doctor for a checkup. Snow Cloud was small but in perfect health. My last blood tests showed nothing wrong but low blood sugar. The strange, malformed blood-cells that had shown up in every test for the past six months had disappeared.

The doctor smiled and said, "I don't know what's happened. You've been very ill. I never could find out what was wrong, and I don't know why you're well. I want you to have a blood test every six months, but as far as I can tell now, you'll live to see your grandchildren."

I had the follow-up blood tests, but the problem never showed up again. The doctor never did know what my illness had been, what had caused it; or why it had disappeared. I didn't know the answer to the first two questions, but I was sure that prayer was the answer to the third.

Life had a new sweetness now that I knew how fragile it was.

SNOW CLOUD

May life bring lovely things your way,
Golden sunsets at the end of day,
A quiet home among tall trees,
A restful soul, a heart at ease.

Let your life be filled with happy hours,
Good books, a hillside of flowers,
Trusted friends all the years through,
And may gentle Jesus richly bless you.

175

Chapter Twenty - One

I was so busy taking care of the three little boys I had isolated myself from the rest of the world. I went six months without seeing or speaking to anyone but Don and the children.

"Don't you want to see other women? Don't you want to go visit some neighbors or something? Don't you need to gossip?" Don asked finally.

I shrugged. "I'm happy with my family and my home. I don't need outsiders."

"I think it would do you good to get out and go somewhere and see someone. Tomorrow I think you should take the car and the children and drive into town and buy groceries."

"But you always buy the groceries, and anything I need I can order from a catalog. I don't want to go to town." I had the feeling I had already lost the argument and that Don's mind had been made up before he had even mentioned the trip to town.

"It will do you good. You won't have any trouble. Just drive into town and take Cloud to the clinic for his checkup and buy some groceries and come home. What could possibly happen?" he reasoned.

That night I hardly slept. I worried about all the things I was sure would happen to me—flat tires, getting lost, and having a wreck were just a few of the milder problems I expected.

"Don't worry, you'll do just fine," my husband said the next morning as he slammed the car door and handed me the keys.

"I still wish you were going along. What if I have trouble?" I pleaded.

"You won't have any trouble. All you are going to do is buy groceries, stop at the doctor's and come home. What could possibly happen?"

"I guess you're right." I started the car and drove away. It was my first time out alone with the children since Cloud had been born, and I wasn't sure I could handle all three of them and still drive and do the shopping. But I smiled to myself. Don was right. What could possibly go wrong?

As I drove into town I saw a MAGIC WATER WAND CAR WASH and decided to wash the car to surprise Don. I had never washed the car before, but I had watched Don do it, and it had looked simple enough.

I pulled into the car wash and drove over the curb. As the car bumped the curb the horn let out a short honk. I got out of the car and picked up the water wand with one hand and put my quarter in the slot with the other. I began squirting water at the car, and the boys began squealing and jumping up and down in the back seat. It was then I noticed the windows were still rolled down. Soap and water covered the back seat and the children.

"Roll up the windows!" I shouted and directed the stream of water onto the trunk of the car.

"I can't!" yelled Antelope, "The handle is covered with soap!"

As I reached for the door to help him, the magic washer wand slipped from my hand and suddenly turned into a wild monster trying to beat our car to death.

Bang! Bang! Bang! It flew through the air and hit the top of our car. I ran around the car trying to catch it, but it was swinging so wildly I couldn't even get close. I jumped into the car and sped out of the car wash before the water wand could

177

smash our windshield. I left the monster thrashing around inside the carwash, banging against the walls and squirting soap and water in every direction. A block away I could still hear the banging. I wondered how long a quarter lasted in a car wash.

I wondered if Don would notice the car was half-washed and hoped the boys' clothes and my dress would dry out before we got to the store.

The trip through the grocery store was uneventful except for the fourteen heads of cabbage that rolled down the aisle after Antelope pulled one out of the bottom row.

Finally all I had to do was to take Cloud to the clinic for a checkup, and then I would be on my way home.

The waiting room was crowded, and every seat was taken. I stood against the wall and held Cloud while Antelope and Deer wandered around the room. They soon had the attention of everyone there and were busy making new friends.

One lady who had a white shawl draped across her lap started talking to Antelope. Suddenly, without warning, Antelope picked up the corner of her shawl, wiped his nose with it, and ran off down the hallway, with Deer close behind.

Praying she wouldn't faint, I hurried over to the horrified woman. I apologized and offered to pay for having her shawl cleaned. She refused and mumbled something about never again telling a child to use a handerchief.

A shrill scream suddenly drew everyone's attention toward the emergency room. A nurse left the desk and headed that direction. A lady next to me said she thought they were treating a child who had been hit by a car.

The noise from the emergency room grew louder.

"It's terrible! Why don't they do something for that child's pain!" one lady said.

I looked around for my sons. They were nowhere in sight,

so I headed down the hallway to search for them. As I passed the emergency room I saw the cause of all the noise and confusion. Deer and Antelope were racing around an examination table, with a nurse and doctor close behind them.

I stepped inside and grabbed them and pushed them into a chair, where I held them by their shirt collars.

"Those are the fastest kids I've ever seen!" puffed the doctor. "There were two other patients ahead of you, but I think I'll see you now."

In a few minutes he assured me that Cloud was in perfect health and there was no need for us to come back for at least a year. I loaded the three boys into the car and headed home.

On the way home I noticed there was a large black car just ahead of me. Suddenly the wheels of my car bounced through a deep puddle and the car came down with a thud. The horn blared. It was stuck! I hit it with my hand a couple of times, hoping to jar it loose and stop the noise, but it continued. When I looked up, I saw that the black car ahead of me was a hearse!

I started to drop back, but the driver of the truck in back of me waved for me to keep going. The road was too narrow and too muddy for me to pull over or to stop without getting stuck. There was nothing to do but follow the hearse with my horn sounding. Mile after mile we bounced down the road—the hearse, me and my horn, and the truck behind.

Finally the road widened enough so that I could pull over and let the hearse go on its way without the accompaniment of my horn. I got out to see if I could find a way to stop the noise.

The truck that had been following me pulled over too, and the driver came up to me. "Why are you honking your horn at that hearse?" he yelled above the noise.

"It's an old Indian custom to drive away evil spirits!" I

179

shouted as I raised the hood. "Do you know how to stop this thing?"

In a few minutes I was quietly on my way home.

When I drove into the yard, Don came out of the house to meet me and help me with the grocery bags. "Did you have any trouble?" he asked as he grabbed some sacks.

"No. No trouble at all," I said and followed him into the house. "After all, what could possibly go wrong?"

I loved my three sons but Don and I would have liked a daughter. I prayed about having another child and felt that God would carry me through.

When Snow Cloud was six months old another child was on the way. This time my health was perfect; there were no problems. I was convinced from the start that a daughter was on her way, and everything I bought was pink.

THE NEW BABY

A new little baby to hold real tight,
A new little baby to keep Mama awake all night.
Daddy just smiled and said with a grin,
"Well, I guess here we go again!"

Two little boys running through the door,
A baby in the crib and one crawling on the floor,
Four little children, the oldest one is four—
We're rich in children so we'll never be poor.

Toys, blankets, and diapers all over the place;
We might be tired but there's a smile on my face.
"Go forth and multiply," was the first command in
the Good Book—
It might have said more, but I've been too busy to
look.

180

Chapter Twenty - Two

"Don't tell me you are expecting another baby!" My friend looked at me and shook her head. "Four children in four years? Haven't you ever heard of family planning?"

"Yes, I've heard of family planning. I planned to have a family, and I'm having one," I said.

She laughed. "You must be crazy!"

I was so angry I was on the verge of tears. With that one thoughtless remark she had spoiled my day and taken the sparkle out of the anouncement of our coming baby.

Why do some people consider it a mistake to have a baby? What is wrong with a world where a baby is considered a burden instead of a blessing? Why do mothers think they have to apolo gize for having babies and loving their families? Why is there so much pressure to work outside the home and "be somebody" and have a career? Why can't motherhood be a career?

I was still biting my tongue as I was hanging out my laundry an hour later. "I don't understand it! I don't understand any of it!" I muttered to myself. I knew it was wrong to be angry, but I felt like a bear protecting her cubs.

My friend had been looking for a job. In my mind I wrote an imaginary newspaper ad. I knew it was not the kind of ad she would ever answer!

WANTED: An attractive, well-kept woman with good educa-

tion and pleasant personality. She must be friendly, cheerful, and willing to work twenty-four hours a day with no pay, no vacations, and no sick leave. She must scrub floors, cook meals, clean house, do laundry and ironing and heavy cleaning. She must be able to stretch a dollar six ways, and wear the same dress five years and still look nice. She must have spare time to read bedtime stories, dry a tear, kiss a skinned elbow, make cookies, and play with small children. She must be a companion to her husband, friend, lover, bookkeeper, nurse, cleaning woman, and gardener. WANTED: A MOTHER.

My anger was gone now. I was truly sorry for my friend who didn't know or understand the rich rewards of being a mother. As I went back to the house I called to my sons, "Come inside for milk and cookies."

They answered with squeals of delight and came running to the house and tumbled through the door. Their chubby, dirty arms wrapped around my neck and pulled me off balance, and the four of us tumbled to the floor with shrieks of laughter.

"We love you, Mommy!" they said and scrambled to the table.

My children. Always a blessing, never a burden.

The baby I carried beneath my heart stirred. Thank You, God, for my children.

There had been tornado warnings out for three hours. It was near midnight when the storm hit. The wind howled with fury and blew the bedroom windowpanes out and rain soaked the bed. I stuffed a pillow in the window and sat on the edge of the bed. My fourth baby was on the way. Don would not be home for hours, and I knew I couldn't wait that long.

We didn't have a telephone, and I didn't have a car. Our

182

nearest neighbor was a mile away. I woke up my three sons, put shoes on them, and put their coats on over their pajamas. They were sleepy, and Snow Cloud was as limp as a dishrag. I picked up Cloud in my arms and handed the flashlight to Antelope. I grabbed Deer's hand, and we started out across the fields to get help.

Antelope aimed the flashlight everywhere except onto the muddy path in front of us. Lightning flashed and lit our way more than the wandering flashlight. The four of us were soaked to the skin by the time we had reached the neighbor's house.

I banged on the door and shouted, and in a few minutes a sleepy-eyed man answered the door.

"Can I borrow your phone? I need to call my husband," I said, pushing the three boys inside out of the rain.

I called the plant where Don worked, and the night watchman promised he would give the message to Don.

"I'd like to help, but my pickup don't run," the man said and yawned.

"I'm all right. Thanks for letting me use your phone," I said and led the boys back out into the dark, rainy night. It took longer to walk the mile back home because I had to carry Cloud in my arms and Deer rode piggyback and the fourth child reminded me constantly that it would soon join us.

When we arrived home again I put dry clothing on all the boys and changed my own clothing. Then I gathered up some blankets and pillows to make a bed in the car for the children. It was a seventy-mile drive to the hospital, and the children could sleep in the back seat.

It usually took my husband an hour to drive home from work, but that night, in spite of the rain, he made it in twenty minutes. As we bundled the children into the car he said. "A tornado

183

touched down two miles from here, and the bridge is out at Twin Oaks. We'll have to ford Spring Creek and go through the hills."

"I won't make it," I said through clenched teeth.

"Yes you will," he said, and the tires spun as we pulled out of the yard.

For the next seventy miles we drove through puddles of water up to the front bumper, we slid through mud, and we sped along winding roads. We crossed the state line and skidded up to a stop in front of the hospital in Siloam Springs, Arkansas.

As my husband left me in the delivery room to go back and take care of the boys, who were bedded down in the waiting room, I waited for words that would help me. I expected him to say, "I love you," or, "I'll be praying for you." Instead he looked at me biting my lips and clenching my fists with pain and said, "Well, have fun, honey."

A short time later our only daughter was born, and her name had already been decided. She was Spring Storm.

The plump nurse handed me my beautiful new baby girl. She was only a few hours old, and I hugged her tightly against me with my heart ready to burst with happiness.

I looked up and saw the nurse watching me as I fed my baby. "Do you have children?" I asked.

"Yes, I had a daughter but I lost her," she answered.

"I'm sorry," I said.

"I don't mean she died. I mean that somehow I just lost her. I was so happy when she was born, but I felt we were too far in debt. So when she was six months old I took a part-time job— just for a couple of months to pay off some bills. The part-time job turned into a full-time job, and the couple of months turned into years. She's eighteen years old, and this week she's getting married, and I don't know her at all. We are strangers, and now she's gone. When she was little she'd beg me to read bedtime stories to her, but I was too tired or too busy and I never seemed to get around to it. I'd always promise her, 'Tomorrow,' but it never came. You know, I can't show you one thing I ever bought with the money I earned working. I didn't really need to work. We could have managed without my small income. I cheated myself and my daughter, and nothing can ever give me back my little baby." She wiped her eyes.

My baby was asleep and the nurse gently picked her up to take her back to the nursery.

"You have a beautiful baby. Don't lose her," she said.

"I won't," I said, and my heart ached for her. As I lay back down I promised myself I would read lots of extra bedtime stories to my baby to make up for that little girl whose mother had always been too busy to read to her.

As we brought Spring Storm home from the hospital Don said, "You've had four babies in four years in four different states. I don't mind if you want to have a souvenir from places you've been, but can't you collect plates or salt and pepper shakers like other women?"

FOR SPRING STORM

Jesus, my shepherd, bless my little bed,
Put an angel on my pillow, where I lay my sleepy
    head.
Brothers and Mommy and Daddy bless.
And tonight give us all sweet dreams and rest.
Keep us safe and with us be,
Until we wake up in Heaven's eternity. Amen.

185

Little Antelope,

Snow Cloud,

Lost Deer,

Spring Storm

A Wish for Spring Storm

Robins and blue skies and butterflies, too —
These are the things I wish for you.
With each sunrise, a day special and new,
Love and laughter and dreams come true.
May sunshine always light your way
And life have all the beautiful surprises of a Christ-
mas Day.

Life suddenly became very busy. There didn't seem to be enough hours in the day to do half the things I needed to get done.

I had just finished setting supper on the table one evening when I happened to glance out the window and see the ducks heading for the pond. I groaned. How did those ducks get out of the chicken coop? I must not have hooked the door after I fed them. I would have to go chase them back into the coop. It was nearly dark, and if I left them outside all night a fox would kill them before morning.

Little Antelope and Deer were busy playing with blocks, and the two babies were in their cribs, so I slipped quietly out the kitchen door and ran toward the pond. As soon as the ducks saw me coming they each went a different direction, quacking and flapping their wings. I chased them around the pond twice and finally cornered them in some tall grass and grabbed two of them. I carried them back to the chicken coop and shoved them inside and locked the door. As I was chasing the other two ducks, I noticed how dark it was getting. I hoped the boys weren't getting into trouble. Catching the ducks was taking longer than I had expected. I finally caught the last two and locked them in the chicken coop and returned to the house.

187

An unexpected stillness greeted me when I walked into the kitchen. It wasn't like the boys to be so quiet. My steps quickened on the way to the living room.

The gory sight before me made my eyes blur. My knees buckled, and I sank paralyzed to the floor.

Antelope stood on the couch, his eyes wide. Clutched in his tiny hand was a kitchen knife. Around his mouth was blood, and the front of his shirt was soaked with blood as if his stomach had been ripped open. Blood formed a pool at his feet. On the floor sat Deer, splashed with blood.

"Oh, God! Don't let them die!" I tried to get back to my feet, but I couldn't move. My heart had stopped beating. My sons had been playing with knives while I was chasing stupid ducks, and now they were both badly hurt. I knew that with all the blood Antelope had already lost, he couldn't live!

I began screaming, "Don! Don! Don! Don!"

I had seen him feeding the rabbits down the hill. He would never hear me so far away. But I had underestimated the shrillness of my screaming. In seconds he burst through the door. He was out of breath from running up the hill.

I pointed across the room to Antelope. I still hadn't stopped screaming. "He's ripped his stomach open! He's dying!"

Don ran to him. "If I can pinch off the artery that's cut, maybe I can get the bleeding stopped until we can get him to the hospital!" He shoved his fingers into the red gore on Antelope's chest and asked, "Why isn't he crying?"

"He's in shock!" I said, struggling at last to my feet but still unable to walk. "He's dying!" I sobbed.

Don pulled his hand away and looked at his fingers and rubbed them together. He reached over and touched Antelope's shirt again and sniffed the red stuff on his hand.

188

"This isn't blood!" he said, and looked around. Then he bent over and picked up something from beside the couch and held it up for me to see.

"It isn't blood. Antelope just helped himself to a quart jar of strawberry jam!" Don took the knife out of Antelope's hand and dropped it with a clink into the empty jar.

Tears of relief streamed down my face as I rushed over and saw that the blood and gore were just red jam. While I had been chasing ducks, Antelope had crawled up on the table and taken a knife and "fed" himself and his brother supper.

Don and I both sank weakly onto the couch. We didn't care that we, too, were now covered with strawberry jam. We burst into laughter and continued laughing for joy over the knowledge that the son we thought we had lost was alive and well.

Antelope and Deer sat on the floor and watched with wonder as their parents laughed until their sides ached.

I remembered the joke Flint and Kansas had played on me years earlier, and I laughed even harder. I had fallen for the same trick twice!

I began mopping up the mess, and as I put the boys' clothing into the washing machine I looked at them again. We were lucky. It could have been blood. The knife had been real enough, and I had been out of the house too long. The nightmare could have been real, but praise God, instead of a terrible tragedy it had turned into a joke, a story we would tell the children when they were older. They would ask to hear it again and again: "Mama, tell us again about the night you thought we'd killed ourselves!"

"Thank You, God," I prayed as I poured bleach into the washer. "Thank you for protecting my children while I was trying to protect a bunch of dumb ducks!"

189

My Son
was alive!

Chapter Twenty-Three

"Anything interesting in the mail?" Don asked as he looked through the pile of bills.

"Reverend McPherson wrote a card today. He asked when I was going to write my book," I laughed.

Don looked up from reading the light bill. "What book?"

"It's a joke between us. He always used to tell me I should write a book about what it's like to be an Indian," I said.

"That's a good idea. Why don't you do it?" he asked.

"I don't know how to write a book," I replied, shrugging.

"How do you know? You've read thousands of books. You know what sounds good and what doesn't. I think you should do it. It might help a lot of Indians—maybe white people, too."

"Do you really think I could do it?" I asked. "I wish I could help people know the truth about what it's like to be an Indian."

"You could do it if you really wanted to. Ask God to help you write it," he said and went back to reading the mail.

Maybe it wasn't really a joke. Maybe I really could write a book. Maybe I would start tomorrow.

Reverend McPherson's words came back to me the next morning. *"When are you going to start your book?"*

I looked out the window. A restless wind was blowing, and it was cold outside.

"Today!" I said out loud. "Today I start my book!"

191

I hurried to the closet and began searching for an ancient typewriter that a friend had thrown out years ago. I had dug it out of her trash and had carried it off with her blessings. I searched through old snow boots, Christmas decorations, and Halloween masks until I found it. The typewriter was covered with dust, and the ribbon was missing, but I wasn't discouraged. I carried my treasure into the kitchen and placed it lovingly on the table.

Fired up with enthusiasm, I drove to town and bought a new typewriter ribbon, a package of carbon paper, and a package of two thousand sheets of typing paper.

I carefully arranged everything on the table and glanced at the clock. It was noon. I still had four hours to write a novel before my husband came home from work.

It took a little while to figure out just how to thread the ribbon, and I found that the *L* key didn't work. But that didn't matter; I would use the number 7 key until I could get it repaired. I would just have to remember that a 7 is an upside-down, backward *L*.

I typed my first sentence.

"Don pu77ed me to him and his 7ips gent7y touched mine."

I leaned back in my chair and read my work. So far, so good. It would be a beautiful love story. All I needed now was a plot and characters and some filling in between the beginning and the climax. I liked the word *climax*; it was a good writer's word. An ordinary person would have said "beginning and end," but a writer like myself would say "climax."

I looked at the clock. I decided to get the roast in the oven so it could be cooking while I created.

Back to work. *Let's see; where was I?*

"Don pu77ed me to him and his 7ips gent7y touched mine." Who knows, maybe this was the start of a best-seller.

Maybe it could sound better. I rewrote. All us famous authors rewrite our manuscripts. That was another good writer's word, *manuscripts*. I'd remember that.

"Don's man7y arms pu77ed me to him and his gent7e kiss sea7ed our 7ove."

That's what I call writing!

That's what I call smoke!

The roast had burned. It had taken all afternoon to polish up that sentence. Oh, well, *Gone with the Wind* wasn't written in a day, and once I got the hang of it I could write faster.

I heard Don's car pull up in front.

Well, I had written enough for that day, anyway. I pulled my "manuscript" out of the typewriter, folded it up, and put it away in my apron pocket. I put the typewriter back in the hall closet.

The roast was burned and nothing else was thawed out. I could make pancakes for dinner. I hadn't washed dishes all day because with all that creating I hadn't had time. We could use paper plates for dinner. I hoped the syrup wouldn't soak through paper plates. Maybe if we ate fast—

I smiled and patted my apron pocket, where my manuscript rested. The next time Reverend McPherson asked when I was going to write a book, I could tell him I had already started!

I would need a pen name. No one would ever read a book written by someone called Crying Wind. I would use a typical white woman's name. I would call myself Gwendolyn Lovequist.

I had to spend the next day digging a peanut butter and jelly sandwich out of the keys after Lost Deer tried to run his sandwich through the roller to "smash it more flat."

Late that night, while the family slept, I began writing a book called *Crying Wind*.

"Moccasined feet moved quietly down the dry arroyo. . . ."

As the pages piled up I found myself weeping as I relived the

193

past. The glory of my horse, Thunderhooves; the death of my grandmother; the long search for the true God. As I struggled to get my thoughts on paper, I wondered if anyone would ever read the words of an uneducated half-breed.

I had underestimated God's plan for my life.

Chapter Twenty-Four

Suddenly my eyes flew open and I was filled with dread as I rolled over and looked at the alarm clock. It was nearly time to get up. I groaned silently and shut my eyes tightly, wishing I could shut out the day. Today was my birthday. I hated birthdays. I hated becoming a year older.

I sighed, climbed out of bed, pulled on my faded pink housecoat, and staggered down the hall. The children were still asleep, so maybe Don and I could have a nice quiet breakfast together for a change. I put on the coffee and scrambled some eggs. The toast had just popped up when he walked into the kitchen.

"Morning," he said, and he reached for a cup of coffee.

He hadn't even looked up at me. I didn't know whether I was glad or mad that he had forgotten my birthday.

Don gulped down his breakfast and grabbed his lunchbox. Kissing me on the cheek, he dashed out the kitchen door and let it slam behind him.

The door slamming sounded like a rifle shot, and I heard a cry from the boys' bedroom. The day had officially begun.

I dropped the sugar bowl on the floor, scattering sugar to the far corners of the kitchen. The angel food cake I baked fell so flat that it looked like a tortilla with a hole in the middle. A sudden shower splashed mud and leaves on my laundry before I could get it off the clothesline, and my son pulled the table-

195

cloth off, taking dishes, food, and all onto the floor with him.

Tears rolled down my cheeks as I mopped the floor for the third time. I growled, "I hate birthdays!"

Lost Deer pulled on my skirt and said, "Don't cry, Mommy, Jesus loves you."

How many times had I said those very words to him? Now he was handing them back to me.

Of course Jesus loved me; I knew that was true. Then why did I become so upset over such small things?

I reviewed the morning. I had gotten up in a bad mood. It had been my own carelessness that had broken the sugar bowl. Had I really followed the recipe for the cake, or had I just guessed at the measurements? I had seen those clouds blowing in from the north; if I had paid attention, I would have had time to get the clothes in off the line before the rain came. All my troubles could have been avoided if I had begun the day in a better mood and had been more careful.

My son's words had reminded me that even when I'm out of sorts, God isn't. Jesus loves me even when I'm grouchy, even when I'm having a bad day, and even when I'm unlovable.

My mind went back to my fifteenth birthday. It was the day of the accident that cost grandmother her life. A few days later my wonderful horse had died, and then I had been abandoned by my favorite uncle. It had been a dark time in my life and had spoiled all the birthdays afterward.

I went to my bedroom and lifted the heavy lid of the old cedar chest. I searched around the bottom until my fingers touched a small box.

I lifted it out and opened the lid. Inside was a small, china horse. The legs were broken off, but it was the horse's head that I cared about. I had seen this figurine in a shop years ago,

196

and my heart had leaped when I saw it. It was the image of Thunderhooves. How I loved this figurine! It had stood proudly on a shelf, with its little glass mane flowing out from an invisible wind. It had made me feel good to look at it. Then one day one of the children had knocked it off, and its legs had broken. I had thrown the broken pieces into the trash, and then later I had dug them out again and wrapped them in a handkerchief. Now I kept the broken pieces in this box. On days when I was restless, I would take out the little figurine and look at the face that reminded me so much of Thunderhooves. It was a secret link with my past.

I thought of my mother and wondered if she remembered it was my birthday. Today memories of my past haunted me, troubling my mind.

When Don came home I was still in a bad mood.

"You forgot my birthday!" I sniffed. "And I'm the only wife you have!"

He laughed. "Have I ever forgotten your birthday?" He opened his lunch box and took out a small package and gave it to me.

I eagerly tore off the paper and found a beautiful turquoise ring. I felt ashamed for scolding him about my birthday.

We spent a rowdy evening wrestling with the children and playing every game we could think of. We were all exhausted by bedtime, and a gentle rain outside made a soft, warm bed a welcome sight even to the children.

The raindrops became larger and fell faster. Lighning tore jagged streaks across the sky, and the thunder crashed so loudly it rattled the windows. The thunder woke up the baby and she cried. I carried her into the next room and rocked her until she fell asleep in my arms.

I looked out the bedroom window. The storm was blowing away. The thunder was only a distant rumble, and the lightning lit up clouds far away.

I put an extra blanket on the baby and tucked her in. "Daddy and me and baby makes three," I whispered, but now there were four babies. "Thank You, God, for my wonderful family." We had come a long way together. How I wished we could go back and do it all again! How sweet life could be.

I drew the curtains and went to bed. The storm was past, and I was grateful my birthday was over and wouldn't return for another year.

I fell asleep quickly, but it was a troubled sleep. I dreamed of a voice calling me over and over, a familiar voice but one I couldn't quite identify. Suddenly in the darkness she appeared! My mother, Little Bird, stood before me, calling my name. I started to run to her, but someone caught my arm and stopped me, saying, "It's too late, she's dead!"

I began to cry, "It's not too late! It can't be too late!"

The grip on my arm became stronger and began shaking me.

"Honey, wake up!" It was Don's voice, and he was shaking me. "You're having another nightmare."

My pillow was wet from tears, and my throat ached. "I saw my mother! She was calling me!" I cried.

He pulled me closer to him and tucked in the blankets. "It was only a dream. Go back to sleep."

"No! I saw her! She was here in this room!"

"It was a dream," he said and went back to sleep.

I got out of bed and turned on the lights. There was no one here but Don and myself. It had only been a dream, but it had seemed so real!

I went back over every word in the dream. What if she really

198

were calling me from somewhere? What if she were dying and the dream had been a warning?

I wiped away my tears and went to my desk for a pen and some paper.

I was going to find my mother. I wasn't going to wait until it was too late, as it had been in the dream.

I had been out of touch with my family since my marriage, partly because I had become a Christian and partly because I had married a non-Indian. It wouldn't be easy to go to them now and ask help in finding my mother. It was possible that none of them knew where she was. She had disappeared a long time ago.

I decided to write to my Aunt Fawn. I was sure she had always known more than she had told.

My letter was short. "Dear Aunt Fawn, Can you help me find my Mother? Love, Crying Wind."

I sealed the envelope and addressed it and slipped into my coat. Holding a flashlight to find my way, I waded through the rain to the mailbox. I knew if I waited until morning I probably wouldn't send the letter, and after all these years I was afraid to wait any longer.

I was shivering as I dropped it into the mailbox. "Please don't let it be too late," I prayed and hurried back inside and snuggled up to Don for warmth.

My mind was at peace. I had taken the first step; now it was out of my hands. The next move was up to Aunt Fawn, and to God.

It was nearly a month before I received an answer from Aunt Fawn. I had nearly given up hope of ever hearing from her and had decided that my search had ended before it had begun.

Dear Crying Wind,

I have not heard from your mother in several years. I think she worked with this lady, she might know where she is. Here is her address,

Aunt Fawn

P.S. I heard you got religion.

I smiled as I read, "I heard you got religion." Everyone in the family had probably heard about Flint's and Cloud's and my becoming Christians. I bet tongues really wagged and heads shook when they spoke of us. I would write to her and try to explain what God had done for me, but right now I wanted to write to the woman who had been a friend of my mother.

Her reply came quickly.

Dear Little Crying Wind,

Your mother spoke of you often when we were together but I lost track of her when she moved to Kansas. I'll enclose the last address I had for her.

Good Luck.

Mrs. Murphy

I felt I was getting close to finding my mother now. The next letter I wrote was to her. I wrote a dozen letters before I decided on a simple, short note.

Dear Little Bird,

I am Crying Wind, your daughter. I am married now and have four children. I would like to hear from you.

Crying Wind

I sent it to the address in Mrs. Murphy's letter, and on the outside of the envelope I wrote "Please Forward," in case she had moved.

Now the hard part began. Days passed with no answer, and I expected my letter to come back marked "Address Unknown." A week later it came.

My Daughter,

Thank you for writing to us. I ask you to forgive me for all the years I wasted. I made many mistakes, my heart breaks because of them. I'm getting old, I wasted most of my life.

Your father and I are together after all those years apart. We both came to know our Savior and we are Christians now.

I wanted to find you but I thought it was too late. You never answered any of the letters I sent to you after I left you with Shima Sani. I thought you hated me too much.

Please, my daughter, write to us again. Do you have a picture I could have?

Do you need help? Please write.

Love,
Mother and Father

I sat down on the floor and wept and read the letter ten times. "We are Christians," she had said, "Your father and I are together." I couldn't believe it! My parents, who had hated each other enough to kill each other, were now together and knew the Lord! It was a miracle!

I puzzled over the line, "You never answered any of the letters." I had never received any letters from my mother. Was it

201

possible that Shima Sani had hidden them from me? She had done many sneaky things in her life; this could have been one of them.

When Don came home I showed him the letter.

"So, you've found your mother," he said and handed the letter back to me. "How do you feel about her?"

"I don't know. I'm glad I found her. I'm happy she and my father are Christians, but it has been such a long time—I really don't know yet how I feel, but I want to know her better."

Don's face looked worried. "Be careful and go slow," he warned.

I nodded. "I'll be careful. I won't expect too much."

I answered her letter and sent her pictures of all of us.

Her next letter held a picture of herself and my father. I looked at it a hundred times. My mother had Grandmother's eyes, black, hooded eyes like an eagle. In twenty years she would be as old and wrinkled as Grandmother had been. I wondered if I would look like my mother in twenty years.

She looked like a gentle, shy creature, like a timid rabbit about to run away and hide. It hurt to see my father looking so old and tired. I hadn't thought about my parents aging; in my mind they had stayed young.

They had married too young, and they had both run away from the unhappy marriage. She had left me with Grandmother because she had thought it was the best thing for me.

Letters traveled back and forth. Sometimes awkward, sometimes funny, often sad, our letters began pulling us back together.

New knowledge came to light. My mother said she had tried to return to me, but Grandmother had forbidden her to come back home. She said she had written to me many times, but her letters had come back unopened.

She repeated often that she had lived to regret her mistakes, and from her letters it was plain that she and my father were really Christians. They had found God just a year earlier, both on the same night, at a revival meeting in their small town.

It would take time to unravel all the knots in our relationship. It's not easy to overcome the hurt and loneliness of so many years.

"Do you want to see your parents?" Don asked.

"Not yet. I think we all feel like we want to take things slow. We need time to get used to each other. No one wants to make a mistake that would spoil things. I think this is our last chance to be—to be friends. When we all feel the time is right, then we'll get together. Right now the letters are enough. They are more than I ever expected to have."

"You know," Don said after he read the last letter, "they sound like the kind of people I'd like to have for friends."

It was a strange feeling to have parents after so many years. It seemed that for so long I had been all alone in the world. Then God had given me friends, a husband, children, and now my parents.

It never fails to amaze me how God can work the impossible.

Chapter Twenty-Five

"My book is going to be published!" I shouted.

"I knew it! I knew it!" Don swung me around the room. "I told you so!"

I praised God for this great blessing, because I knew that I had no talent of my own and He was responsible.

When I told Reverend McPherson my book *Crying Wind* was going to be published, he smiled and said, "I knew it."

I laughed, "That's what Don said."

"Don and I had faith in you. We've come a long, hard way together." He took my hand and prayed that the book would be a success and that it would touch lives and save souls. "I wish Audrey could have shared this day," he said.

I want to read the dedication to you," I said, and began reading in a shaky voice,

> "For Rev. Glenn O. McPherson
> Because he believed in me,
> I learned to believe in myself"

He shook his head, and his eyes filled with tears.

"I can't speak. I can't tell you—Thanks."

Many kind and encouraging letters came. When the publisher asked if I could go on some tours with the book, I said I couldn't go. "I don't have anything to say. Besides, I can't leave my family," I explained.

"We could arrange very short tours so you wouldn't be away from your family more than a few days at a time. We know the family comes first. Say what is in your heart, Crying Wind. Tell the people the truth about the Indians. Tell them the Indian religion is not beautiful—that no religion is beautiful unless it has the living God as the center."

"I can't talk in front of people. I get afraid," I said, feeling like Moses.

"You don't have to be afraid. You will be speaking for God, and He will help you. Someone needs to speak for the Indians. Why not you?"

I looked to Don for direction.

"It's the chance of a lifetime. I can take care of the children. You have to go. I want you to," he said.

"I'll go," I said.

I prayed for God's help for the months ahead. I would be in a strange new world of airplanes, travel, and skyscrapers. Wherever I would go, whether to a reservation in New Mexico or to a hotel in New York, my message would be the same: the Indian needs God, and so does everyone else.

I couldn't believe God had taken such an unimportant nobody as myself and given me the opportunity to share my story with thousands of people across the country. You never know what God can do until you let go of your life and let Him take over.

Chapter Twenty-Six

Our farm was a beautiful place, but the tornados and flash floods frightened me. I watched for snakes constantly and lost count of how many I killed. Each day I prayed, "God, protect my children from snakes while they play outside." The tarantulas made me nearly faint when I saw them, and the scorpions sent me running.

I missed the mountains and the forests of pine and aspen. I missed my church and my friends. I was homesick. I spent most of my time thinking about old friends and old times.

While I was hanging out the laundry one morning, homesickness engulfed me like a tidal wave, and I fell to my knees and cried out, "I want to go home! I want to go home!" Over and over I said it until it was no longer a wish or desire but a desperate prayer.

Don wasn't as happy with the farm as he had been, and when I told him how much I wanted to go back home he decided to sell the farm.

It was harder to leave the farm than I thought it would be. I had never been satisfied with it; it was as if something had always been missing, something I couldn't put into words. It had never really seemed like home to me. But now, as we packed to leave, I felt the grief I would have felt if a friend had died. I was losing something. We had made memories here. Our children had been babies here. What if we could never find another home, and we wandered around forever? I was afraid, terribly afraid, and wondered if my homesickness was going to make my family pay a terrible price. It would mean a new start. Don would have to find new work, the children would leave friends behind.

"God, help us," I prayed as we drove away, leaving our farm behind.

PRAYER FOR A NEW HOME

God, give us a little home
From which we'll never roam,
A fireplace and soft chairs,
Four cozy, little beds upstairs,
Just a few acres of ground,
With tall trees standing all around,
Mountains and rocks and blue sky above,
Lots of laughter, lots of love,
Soft winds to blow, soft rains to fall,
God, bless our home and family and all,
Kittens, toys, books and balls,
Games and teddy bears and dolls,
A garden with some pretty flowers,
Children playing and laughing for hours.
Give us a home, and we'll do our best,
To make You the honored Guest.

When we arrived in Colorado, we found a small place to rent while Don hunted for work and I searched for a home.

Flint and Cloud now had small ranches up in the high mountains. Flint and his wife had two sons; Cloud and his wife had two daughters. They all led quiet, Christian lives.

Cloud came to visit and handed Little Antelope the small bow and arrows he had made with his own hands. "Here, little warrior, go kill a bear," he laughed.

"I will shoot a hundred bears!" Little Antelope boasted and ran off with his new toy.

"That was a beautiful gift, Cloud. It took you a lot of time to make it, and he will remember it after he is grown." I thanked him.

Cloud shrugged. "It's nothing." But I could see he was proud of his work.

"Cloud, I've written a book," I said timidly.

"What about?" he asked.

I swallowed hard. "About us."

He looked up.

"I wrote about us, our family, about everything," I said weakly.

"Everything?" he asked.

"Yes."

He was silent for a moment. Then he smiled. "Good for you!" he said, and he slapped my back so hard I staggered under the blow. "It's about time somebody in this family did something. I'm proud of you!"

A big weight slid from my shoulders and I stood taller.

He looked back at Little Antelope, who was trying out his new bow.

"You know, Cry, there will be those who will be against you. Some in the family won't like you telling about Indian ways. They will be angry with you. It could even be dangerous. You will be called some bad names. They will say you are a liar, to make themselves look better. It is going to be hard for you."

"I've thought about that. But I felt in my heart I was doing the right thing. Our people have lived in darkness too long—

too many secrets, too much fear. It's time to throw open the windows and let some light into our lives and sweep out the ancient dust of the old ways," I said.

"I'm with you, Cry, but those who walk on the old trails will fight you," he warned.

"If you're behind me, Cloud, I can face the others," I said.

I soon found that a clear line was drawn through the family. Those who had become Christians liked the book; those who followed the old religion hated the book and hated me for writing it.

If my book did nothing else, I hoped it would tell people the truth so they would stop saying, "The Indian religion is beautiful. Let's leave them alone."

Leave them alone, so they can live without hope? Leave them alone, so they will never know the forgiveness of sin or the love of God? Leave them alone, so they can die in darkness and go to a Godless grave? What is beautiful about that?

Don and I looked at dozens of houses. Most of the ones with acreage were too expensive for us, but we knew we wouldn't be happy living in the city because we needed "breathing room."

A friend sent a real estate agent over to meet us. "I'm T. J. Calhoun, and I'm going to find you a home!" he smiled.

T. J. showed us several places in our price range, but nothing was quite right.

I was becoming discouraged and Don was growing impatient to be settled. He had found a job as a truck driver making local deliveries, and although the hours were long and the pay was low, we were grateful he had found work so quickly when so many people were unemployed. Now all we needed was a home, a real home.

I was feeling guilty for uprooting my family and bringing

209

them here and now having us homeless and unsettled. It seemed impossible that we would ever find the kind of home we wanted for the small amount of money we had.

T. J. came by late one afternoon. "I have one place I haven't shown you." He hesitated. "It's my own place. I guess I didn't want to let it go yet, but I know I have to. Your life changes; you have to let go of the past and make a new start."

He drove us slowly over the dusty, twisting, mountain roads, "It was an old homestead surrounded by national forest, and I sold all but eleven acres and the house and barns. Now I guess it's time to let go of the last piece." He left the main road and drove half a mile through thick forest.

The sun was just setting as T. J. drove up to the old wooden gate. "We'll have to walk in from here," he said.

We climbed out of the truck and walked up the twin ruts that led through the rocks in the road.

As we walked around a bend, I saw the ranch for the first time, and tears filled my eyes. The log cabin and log barns were nearly a hundred years old. Tall pines and huge rocks surrounded the ranch and kept it hidden from view in a safe little valley.

When we stepped inside the cabin we found a huge fireplace, beamed ceilings, and lamps mounted on wagon wheels.

"We'll take it!" I said.

Don broke into a fit of coughing, and T. J.'s face went pale.

That night Don gave me several lectures on how not to buy a house and how we couldn't possibly afford T. J.'s old ranch.

"Offer him less than he's asking," I begged. "I have to have that place! It's my home!"

"He won't take less now that he knows you want it. You should have kept quiet, kept him guessing." He changed the

210

subject. "That little goat farm near here isn't so bad, and we can afford it."

"It's awful. The goats have killed most of the trees. There's no heating system. No! No! I want my home!" I cried. "God wouldn't have shown me that ranch to tease me. He meant for me to have it!"

The next day Don went to T. J. and offered him thousands of dollars less than he was asking for the ranch. Much to his amazement, T. J. accepted.

We had our home! It didn't take us long to move into Thundering Hills, our own hidden valley, our own refuge from the outside world.

Home again. Each Sunday we sat in our church, where dear Reverend McPherson was still pastor, and our hearts were lifted with his messages of God's love.

I looked around the church. Sally was still there, but many faces were gone. Audrey, Edythe, and many others had been called to glory. Where I had once sat alone, I now sat with my family, and we filled an entire pew.

Reverend McPherson stood in the pulpit. The years had made him a little grayer, a little more humble, and a little more precious to us.

Chapter Twenty-Seven

How I loved autumn! God touching the trees and turning them to gold, and the leaves falling down on me like blessings from heaven! I loved catching the leaves in my hands and swishing through piles of them with my feet. What a pleasure to watch the children tumble and roll in the crispy, crunchy leaves until they had leaves covering them and clinging to their clothing and hair. Autumn was special. Nature seemed to work extra hard making the mountains beautiful so we would have pretty pictures to hold onto in our memories through the hard, cold winter.

It had always been my favorite season, but this year I dreaded the end of summer because I knew the sweet days of innocence and freedom would be snatched away from my eldest son, who was now old enough to enter school.

The very word *September* sent a cold shadow over my heart. The end of summer and the beginning of trouble.

"I won't send my son to school!" I said too loudly. "School is a terrible place! The teachers are cruel, hateful people who enjoy embarrassing and humiliating small children!" My mind flooded with painful memories of my own schooldays. It was a nightmare I had relived often. No! I wouldn't let my children be laughed at. My children would not be chased home by gangs of children taunting them. No! My children would not go to school!

"The law says we have to send our children to school," my husband said firmly.

"The law has no right to take my children from me!" I said through tears. "It is legalized kidnapping!"

"They aren't taking your children away from you. They want every child to have an education. He will only be gone a few hours each day," Don said. "Why are you so angry?"

"I'm more than angry! I'm mad and sick! I want to fight, but there is no way to fight. The government says they need an education, but they don't teach them what they need to know. Does the school teach them about God? No! Does the school teach them how to cook or hunt or how to survive in the wilderness? No! Does it teach them how to be good people or how to care for a family? No! They teach Johnny ate six apples and how many are left. They say a white man named Columbus discovered America, but the Indians had discovered America thousands of years earlier. They teach Custer was massacred by the Indians, but Custer was a cowardly glory-hunter who butchered women and babies! They teach lies!" I shouted. "I can teach them at home. I'll buy books. The government has no right to take my children! I will fight them!"

My husband smiled. "An Indian, more than anyone else, should know you cannot fight the government."

I wilted. I knew he was right. You cannot fight the government and win. My son would have to go to school. I was sending my lamb to the slaughter.

I ran from the room and sought refuge in the forest. I sat under a dead tree and wept bitterly as I saw my children suffering the same agony I had suffered.

It wasn't fair! My heart was on fire. I would take my children and run away. We would go back to the reservation, where people would not care whether or not my children went to

213

school. They had been through the same treatment at the white man's school, and they would understand.

I remembered my uncles speaking of the "education" the government had given them. A bus had come to the reservation, and children were dragged screaming out of their homes and put on the bus. They were driven away to Indian boarding schools, where they were kept in dormitories. They didn't see their families again until the end of the school year, because the school was far from their homes and their families didn't have money for transportation. They couldn't even communicate by mail, because many of the parents could not read or write. Often neither parent nor child knew if the other was even alive.

Many of the teenagers would jump out the emergency doors of the buses and run across country and hide to escape. Then the buses began showing up with leg chains, and the runaways were shackled into the bus seats until they were "safe" at school. It wasn't until recently that schools were built on the reservations so the children could return to their homes each night instead of being kidnapped for months at a time.

My own tribe, the Kickapoo, had fought education more than any other tribe, burning down six different schools that the government had built to force change on the young people. No tribe has held onto its old ways more than the Southern Kickapoo. They are nearly all illiterate, not because they are stupid but because they refuse to learn the "white man's way" of doing things. They choose *not* to be educated.

I ran out of tears. I took several deep breaths. The evening air would clear my thoughts. There was a way to win; there is always a way to win if you can just think of it.

Little Antelope would have to go to school. The law said so. If I didn't take advantage of the "free" education, I would be put into prison. The law said— But if a child is sick, even the law cannot force him to go! I smiled. Yes, Little Antelope would miss much school. I would just say he was sick and keep him home most of the time. It would be easy. I stood up and brushed the dirt off my clothes. I felt better now. I would send him to school a few days and keep him home a few days. It was settled.

The next day my heart was heavy as I drove my small five-year-old son to school. He was dressed in his new blue jeans and a new shirt. His eyes were shining with eagerness. I watched him as I drove him to school. He was excited. He didn't understand he would soon find out that school was not fun, teachers were not your friends, and other children did not play with half-breeds. The lessons he would learn this day would hurt for many years to come.

I drove as slowly as I could, but too soon we arrived at the school. I tried to ignore the knot in my stomach as I took his small hand in mine and led him inside the building.

A frightened child was pushed into the room by his mother. She said a few quick words, looked at her watch, and hurried away, leaving the child alone and terrified in a strange new world. The child began to sob and covered his eyes with chubby little hands.

A thin woman with shiny blue stuff on her eyelids was sitting behind a desk.

"Hello," I said, "This is my son—"

"Fill out these forms, go to room 2A, and Mrs. Jones will take care of you." She shoved a handful of papers across her desk and went on checking her list without even looking at us.

I picked up the papers and sat down at a table to fill them out. Little Antelope clung to my hand as if he were drowning.

I read the forms. *"Name of pupil—"*

"Little Antelope Stafford," I wrote. Then I looked around. All the children were white. I erased the name. "Aaron Staf-

215

ford," I wrote. It would be easier for him to be called Aaron
here. I felt guilty for letting them push me into their little
niche.

"*Address—*"

"Wagon Tongue Gulch."

"*Age—*"

"Five."

"*Race—*"

What difference did it make? I was not ashamed to be an
Indian, but I didn't feel I should have to declare it as if it were a
handicap. *I am Chinese, I am from the moon, I am purple!* I
debated a moment. If I wrote "Indian," I would deny his father.
If I wrote "White," I would deny myself as his mother. If I
wrote "Indian/Caucasian," I would label him a half-breed.
I was tempted to write "Peppermint" (red and white). I considered leaving the space blank. No, that would make me look as
if I didn't know what my son was. I wrote, "American."

I erased my son's name again, and in bold letters I wrote,
"AARON LITTLE ANTELOPE STAFFORD." We were who
we were. The school would not bully me or my children into
being someone else. I picked up the papers in my right hand,
and with my left hand I led my small son to room 2A.

A woman in a brown suit glanced at my papers. "You're in
the wrong place. Go to room 1B.

We walked down the hall to another room. A short woman
in a pantsuit took the papers and looked them over.

"Little Antelope?" She raised her eyebrows.

I looked her straight in the eye without speaking.

"Yes, well—" She read some more and flashed her teeth, but
it was not a smile.

A few minutes later I left Little Antelope in the school and
drove away trying not to think of the terrified look on his face

as I left him with strangers for the first time in his life. Strangers who thought him of less value than themselves because he was different. Strangers who didn't care about him, who thought of him as the boy in desk number four.

Anger raged in my heart. School had not changed; it was still the same, impersonal, spirit-breaking system. I dreaded the days ahead when my son would come home from school crying because of names he had been called. I knew that "half-breed" was probably the kindest he would hear. I knew he would be the target of cruel jokes about Indians, knew he would be bullied into fights he didn't want and would probably lose because he was small for his age and illness had kept him thin.

All I could do was try hard to make his home happier. His home would become a hiding place for him. We were a family, and as long as we stuck together and closed our ranks against "them," we could survive. I hated school for keeping my child a prisoner so many hours each day. It was as if a huge bear were chewing my son into little pieces, grinding him into nothing in its powerful jaws, and sending him home stripped of his identity. The school would spend hours each day stealing his personality, and I would spend hours each night trying to put him back together again.

I watched the clock all day. The hands moved so slowly I thought the day would never end. I cooked Antelope's favorite food for dinner and made cookies, trying to make his first day of school special. Maybe he would come home happy. Maybe everything would be all right. Maybe school had changed.

At last it was four o'clock! I drove the truck down the road and waited for the big, yellow school bus to come bumping along in a cloud of dust.

Antelope climbed off the bus and ran to the truck like a bird set free from its cage. His face was streaked from tears. The pocket was torn off his shirt. My heart sank, because without asking, I knew what had happened.

"I'm happy you are home again." I tried to sound cheerful. "I made cookies for you today." And finally the question, "How was school?"

"A big boy shoved me down on the playground," he said and then silently looked out the window.

When we drove into the yard, and when he saw his brother Deer waiting for him he smiled. "I have friends at home. I don't need friends at school," he said, and he ran to his brother.

I picked up his coat and his lunch box to carry them into the house, and I noticed the lunch box was heavy. I opened it and found his lunch untouched. He had been too nervous to eat a single bit of food.

Don came in to wash up for supper. "How did school go to-day?" he asked and slung a wet towel back on the rack.

I gave him a stormy look. "Well, how do you think it went!" Somehow I blamed him. He was the man of the family—he should have protected his son, he should have done something.

After dinner I began packing Antelope's lunch box for the next day and he came into the kitchen for another cookie.

"What are you doing?"

"Getting things ready for school tomorrow," I answered.

"But I already went! I don't have to go back again, do I?"

"Yes, you have to go back many times," I said.

"But I don't want to go back! Don't make me go back!" he begged and grabbed me around the legs. "Please, Mommy!"

I picked him up and hugged him. "The first day is always hard. Tomorrow will be easier. Maybe tomorrow you will find a friend."

He wiped his eyes. "Do you think so?"

218

"Sure. You won't be afraid tomorrow. You'll do better. You won't be too nervous to eat your lunch."

"I don't want lunch," he said.

"You'll get hungry," I said.

"I can't eat when I'm alone," he answered.

"But you eat with the other children, you aren't alone," I said.

"Yes, I am. I have to eat in a room all alone."

Little Antelope –

"They make me eat alone!"

"What do you mean?" I asked.

"All the children eat in the lunchroom, but the teacher makes me eat in a room by myself."

"There must be someone else in the room with you." He just couldn't be right, he couldn't be eating alone.

"No, the teacher said there wasn't room for me in the lunchroom and I have to eat in another room. I can't eat when I'm alone. My throat closes up and I can't swallow," he said.

"Were you in trouble? Were you being punished?" I asked.

"No, I didn't do anything. I wasn't bad. She doesn't like me."

"I'm sure she likes you. There is a misunderstanding. I will send a note with you tomorrow. I will tell her you must eat with the other children in the lunchroom."

He smiled. "Then I can eat with the other children?"

"Yes, tomorrow will be a better day." I watched him grab a cookie and run off to find his brother.

I wrote a note and put it inside his lunch box.

Dear Mrs. Matthews,

Antelope is very unhappy about eating alone. Please let him eat with the other children.

It would be all right. We had got off to a bad start, but it would get easier.

The next day when he came home from school I was relieved to see his shirt wasn't torn and his face wasn't streaked with tears.

"Today was better, wasn't it?" I asked.

"Yes, nobody shoved me down. I found a piece of green glass on the playground." He dug it out of his pocket and showed it to me. "I found some other treasures, too." He took a bent nail, a broken pencil, and a gum wrapper out of his pocket.

"Those are nice," I said.

"I look for treasures while the other kids play games." He shoved them back into his pockets.

"Don't you play games?" I asked.

"They won't let me. When I try to play, they just push me away. I don't care. I'll just hunt treasures."

I wanted to scream. The other children played games while my son went off by himself and hunted pieces of broken glass and bent nails!

"Isn't there a teacher on the playground with you?" Maybe she didn't know how the children were treating Antelope.

"Yes, Mrs. Matthews was there."

"What did she say?" I asked.

"She told me to stay off the swings."

I was too angry to speak.

The next morning I drove Antelope to school and went into his room. There sat Mrs. Matthews. She showed me her teeth again but it was still not a smile.

I hoped my voice wouldn't sound too angry when I spoke.

"My son says he has to eat his lunch in a room alone."

"Yes," she said, "there is no room for him at the table. It is a very small lunchroom."

"Then there is room for all the children except one?" I asked.

"Yes, that's right."

"Then the children could take turns. My son could eat alone one day, and then another child could eat alone the next day," I suggested.

"No, that wouldn't work. The other children all know each other and are used to eating together," she said.

"But my son will never know the other children if he is in a room by himself," I argued.

"He will adjust. After all, that's what school is all about—adjusting," she said, as if I were five years old.

"He can't eat when he is alone," I repeated.

"He will learn. Perhaps he hasn't any discipline at home," she said, and her blue eyes looked like ice.

"He is very good at home," I said. "He seldom needs discipline."

"Mothers don't always see things from a teacher's point of view," she responded.

"Maybe not. I am not perfect. My son is not perfect." I wanted to add, "Teachers are not perfect," but thought better of it. "I do not want my son punished by making him eat alone. Find another way to punish him if he is in trouble."

"He is not being punished. There just isn't any room for him at the table."

I thought to myself, *He is being punished for having an Indian mother.*

"I think you could find room for him at the table," I said.

"I'll see what I can do." She showed me her teeth again and I left.

"Please, God," I prayed, "let this be the end of it. Let Little Antelope eat with the other children."

Days passed. Nothing changed. Each day Little Antelope brought his lunch home untouched. Each day he had been sent to a room to eat by himself.

I sent more notes to school asking that he be allowed to sit with the other children. None of my notes were answered.

Two weeks passed. My patience was gone.

"Why isn't Antelope in school?" Don asked one morning. "He's missed three days."

When I said I had stopped sending him, the dam burst.

222

"What do you mean you stopped sending him to school?" he shouted.

"The teacher makes him eat in a room alone. I talked to her. I wrote notes. She won't listen. She just says, 'There is no room for your son at the table,'" I explained. "I won't send him to school unless he eats with the other children."

Don stood in silence a minute. Then he stomped across the floor so hard that the house shook, and the windows rattled when he slammed the door behind him.

I looked out the kitchen window and watched as he threw boards and a hammer and a bag of nails into the back of his pickup truck. His tires spun as he sped out of the yard.

In an hour he returned and came into the house. His boots were no longer stomping, and he looked pleased with himself.

"Where were you?"

"I was visiting school. I told Mrs. Matthews that if there wasn't room for my son at the table I would build him a table of his own to eat at, and to show me where to put it. Before I took the second board off the truck she said there would be room at the table for Antelope from now on. Send him back to school tomorrow."

The next day when Antelope returned from school my first question was, "Where did you eat lunch today?"

He smiled broadly. "I ate in the lunchroom with the other children!"

We had won the first round, but it was only the beginning. There would be many battles ahead. We would win a few, but we would lose most of them. We had to fight for the rights that other people take for granted.

Each night I would pray for God to protect my children at school—to protect them from the children who were cruel and especially to protect them from the teachers who could do so much harm. I prayed that someday it would be possible to send my children to a Christian school, where they would be cared for and loved and understood, and where they wouldn't have to fight for the right to eat at a table because there would always be room for them.

In my mind I pictured the perfect teacher and named her Mrs. Baker. She would be kind and understanding. She would love children. *Please, Lord, send me a Mrs. Baker someday to teach my children.*

THE PERFECT TEACHER

Mrs. Baker, thank you.

Thank you for greeting my son with a smile to start
    his day off right,
For protecting him against bigger boys who try to pick
    a fight.
Thank you for helping him unbutton his coat and take
    off his hat,
And for making sure he's bundled up warm when you
    send him home. I appreciate that.
Thank you for your patience and loving concern,
For being firm but not too stern.
Thank you for caring enough to tell him when he's
    wrong,
And for teaching him some prayers and songs.
Thanks for teaching him to say "May I?" and
    "Please,"
And for showing him his ABC's.
If I have to share my son with another woman who's
    new,

I'm glad that "Other Woman" is you.
You're setting the cornerstone for his future by what
    you teach;
It's up to you how far he'll reach.
So please tell my son to reach for a star.
And thanks again for being the kind of teacher you
    are!

Sticks and stones may break my bones but names can never hurt me. No, not true. Names do hurt, names are important. God knew names were important when he told Adam to name all the animals, and later God changed people's names when the direction of their lives changed.

My son was playing outside with a neighbor boy when I heard "Half-breed!"

I opened the back door and invited them inside for refreshments.

"Yes," I said, "Little Antelope, Lost Deer, Snow Cloud, and Spring Storm are half-breeds. That only means they are half Indian and half white. You know what it means to be white. Do you know what it means to be an Indian?" I asked.

The bully and his two friends shrugged and followed Antelope inside.

I handed each child a blanket to wrap himself in and seated them in a circle on the floor.

"Would you like some Indian food?" I asked, and they eagerly nodded.

I passed around popcorn, peanuts, potato chips, hot chocolate, and molasses cookies.

"This isn't Indian food," the bully snorted.

"Yes, it is. Indians grew these foods hundreds of years before the white man ever came to our country. We also had maple syrup, potatoes, gum, and a hundred other foods."

"I didn't know that," the bully said, and he stuffed more popcorn into his face.

I told them the legend of the Thunderbird and sang a song about Geronimo, and suddenly they were full of a dozen questions about Indians.

Just as they started out the door I took a rubber ball out of one boy's hands. "We invented the rubber ball a thousand years ago," I said and handed it back.

"Wow!" He whistled and ran after my son.

"Hey, Little Antelope! Do you think you could give me an Indian name too? Can I be your blood brother? Have you ever lived in a real tepee?" His voice faded away as they ran across the yard.

I shut the door and picked up the blankets off the floor.

The bully probably wouldn't call Little Antelope half-breed again. Right now he was too busy wishing he were part Indian. Today's problem was taken care of with a few cookies and some legends.

Someday he again would be called half-breed, and it would keep him from marrying the girl he loved or it would keep him from getting the job he wanted. Then a handful of cookies wouldn't make the hurt go away.

Please, God, be near him on the days people call him half-breed and worse names. Son, be proud of what you are. You can have the best of both worlds. You have a choice—when you grow up you can live like an Indian and walk a forest path, or you can live like a white man and follow the paved highway. Choose the one that makes you happy. Be proud, always be proud of having two bloods in your veins!

226

Chapter Twenty-Eight

Because of my children I was able to catch glimpses of the kindness and tenderness of God that couldn't be preached in a thousand sermons. Children seem to know more about God than anyone, and by listening to them, I could hear God speaking to me.

Little Antelope came running into the house with the pieces of a broken truck clutched in his little hands.

"Fix it, Mommy," he cried.

The wheels had slipped out of their grooves. It would be simple to fix it—all I had to do was snap them back into the slots.

"It's all right, I can fix it," I said, but as soon as I reached for the toy, my son's fingers tightened around it.

"Fix it, Mommy!" he sobbed.

He handed me the truck but kept the wheels.

"Son, you have to give me all the pieces, or I can't fix it."

Suddenly I knew that I had been asking God to "fix" my problem, but I hadn't turned over all the pieces. Now I knew I had to turn the whole thing over to God.

"Casting all your care upon him; for he careth for you" (1 Peter 5:7). Don't cast some of your cares, or a few cares, cast *all* your cares.

My son handed the wheels to me, and in a second I snapped

them, into place. The toy was as good as new, and he went back to his play.

I couldn't help him until he had trusted me enough to give me all the pieces. I hadn't been trusting God with all the pieces of my life. I was going to do better.

When I hung up our new picture of Jesus standing at the door and knocking, Deer was greatly impressed.

Later that day there was a heavy rainstorm, and a loud crash of thunder shook the house and rattled the windows. My son's eyes grew big and round, and he looked at me and asked, "Is that Jesus knocking at our door?"

I explained to him that it was only thunder, but he wouldn't believe me until I opened the door and showed him there was no one there.

How real Jesus is to a child! How sure my son was that Jesus would be standing on our porch. Somehow, even at his early age, he sensed that the knock of Jesus on the door would sound different than an ordinary knock. Somehow His knock would contain power and strength, and perhaps even sound like thunder.

Would I know when Jesus knocked on my heart, or was I too busy? Was I close enough to hear His whispered messages, or did He have to beat my door down to get my attention?

Now when I feel a tug on my heart or conscience I ask myself, "Is that Jesus knocking?" "Behold, I stand at the door, and knock: if any man hear my voice, and open the door, I will come in to him, and will sup with him, and he with me" (Revelation 3:20).

Antelope spilled his bowl of cereal on the floor. Lost Deer took a crayon and scribbled all over the mirror. Cloud tried to climb up the drapes, and the nails pulled out of the wall, and drapes, curtain rods, son, and all came crashing to the floor. While I was trying to rehang the curtains, the boys went into the kitchen.

Knowing they were being far too quiet, I called, "What are you doing?"

Antelope was quick to answer. "Nothing, Mama. We are just trying to put the eggs back together."

I dropped the drapes and hurried into the kitchen. They had broken a dozen eggs on the floor to see if they were all alike inside, and now they were trying to scoop the runny, raw eggs back into the shells before I found out what they had done.

Although I was upset over the waste of good food and the awful mess, still I laughed at their efforts to hide their crime. There is just no way in the world to put an egg back together again!

Sometimes I get into trouble and try to put things back together again, hoping God won't notice what I've done wrong. My efforts to hide my sins from Him are just as useless as my sons' efforts to hide broken eggs from me.

"For there is nothing covered, that shall not be revealed; neither hid, that shall not be known" (Luke 12:2).

How proud I was of my new rosebush! On each branch, huge, pink buds were swelling, just waiting to burst into full, beautiful roses.

Each day the children and I would walk out and look at the bush and look forward to when it would finally be covered with blooms.

One morning Antelope reached the rosebush ahead of me, and I could see he was carefully peeling back the protecting green leaves and patiently prying open each little petal.

229

"What are you doing?" I asked, trying not to sound too worried about my flowers.

"I'm trying to help the roses bloom without bruising the petals," he said seriously.

I told him nature couldn't be hurried, and the rose would bloom in its own good time.

As I tucked him into bed that night and saw how tiny and fragile he was, I breathed a silent prayer, *Please, Lord, teach me to help my children bloom without bruising their petals.*

"Train up a child in the way he should go: and when he is old, he will not depart from it" (Proverbs 22:6).

Today Little Antelope picked some dandelions for me. He held them so tightly the stems were nearly crushed, and there were beads of sweat on his forehead from running in the hot summer sun.

"I love you, Mama. I picked these sunshine flowers for you," he said as he handed them to me.

Sunshine Flower

"Like father, like son." I smiled as I remembered the day many years ago when his father had handed me "sunshine flowers." I gave him a kiss. It takes a special kind of person to see beauty everywhere. Even a common weed becomes beautiful when love touches it.

Lost Deer had been asking for a puppy for over a month, but his Daddy kept saying, "No dogs! A dog will dig up our garden, chase our ducks and kill our rabbits. No dog, and that's final!"

Each night Lost Deer prayed for a puppy, and each morning he was disappointed not to find one waiting outside.

I was peeling potatoes for dinner, and he was sitting on the floor at my feet asking for the thousandth time, "Why won't Daddy let me have a puppy?"

"Because they are a lot of trouble. Don't cry. Maybe he will change his mind someday," I encouraged him.

"No he won't, and I'll never have a puppy in a million years!" he wailed.

I looked into his dirty, tear-streaked face and couldn't deny his one wish, so I said the words that were first spoken by Eve. "I know a way to make Daddy change his mind."

"Really?" Lost Deer wiped away his tears and sniffed.

I handed him a potato. "Take this and carry it with you until it turns into a puppy," I whispered so no one else would hear. "Never let it out of your sight for one minute. Keep it with you all the time, and on the third day, tie a string around it and drag it around the yard and see what happens!"

Lost Deer grabbed the potato with both hands. "Mama, how do you make a potato into a puppy?" He turned it over and over.

"Sh! It's a secret!" I whispered and sent him on his way.

Lord, you know what a woman must do to keep peace in her home! I prayed.

Lost Deer faithfully carried his potato around for two days. On the third day I said to Don, "We must get a pet for Lost Deer."

"What makes you think he needs a pet?" Don leaned against the doorway.

"I'm afraid he's getting an emotional problem," I said. "He's been carrying a potato around with him for days. He calls it Skipper and says it's his pet. He takes it to bed with him, he gives it baths, and right now he has a string tied to it and he's dragging it around the yard."

"A potato?" Don looked out the window at Deer taking his potato for a walk.

"It will break his heart when the potato gets mushy and rots." I put away the last of the dishes. "Besides, every time I try to peel potatoes for dinner, Deer cries because he says I'm killing his pet's family."

"A potato?" Don queried. "My son has a pet potato?"

"Well, you said he couldn't have a puppy, and I think it was such a terrible disappointment that something snapped in his poor little mind, and he's probably having a nervous breakdown," I said.

"He's only three years old!" Don said. "Three-year-old kids don't have nervous breakdowns!"

"Then why is he dragging a potato around the yard on a string?" I asked.

"I'll bring home a puppy tomorrow," he said and walked outside to look for Deer. As the door slammed I heard him say once more, "A pet potato?"

The next day Don brought home a wiggling puppy and two pregnant cats that soon blessed us with fourteen kittens.

Everyone was happy. Don thought he had saved his son from a nervous breakdown. Lost Deer had his puppy (and sixteen

232

cats), and he believed his Mother could change a potato into a puppy. And I was happy because I got back my potato and cooked it for our dinner.

Blessed are the peacemakers!

In the back of my mind, though, there was a small voice that kept reminding me that I had played a trick on my husband and hadn't been honest with him. True, I had convinced him to get Lost Deer his puppy, but I wished I had found another way to do it. What had begun as a simple thing had grown, and it made my heart feel heavy. I wondered if I should confess my deception to Don and tell him I was sorry.

At dinner one evening Little Antelope said, "Daddy, I saw a little black pony at the Oak's Farm today. He was sure pretty. Daddy, can I have a pony?"

The room grew quiet as all eyes were on Don. He laid down his fork and put his hand on Little Antelope's shoulder.

In an exaggerated whisper he said, "Son, if you want a pony, this is how you get it. First, take a large watermelon, tie a string around it and drag it around the house—"

I knocked over my glass of iced tea and began choking. "How did you know?" I gasped.

Don laughed, "When I gave the puppy to Lost Deer he told me that you had said you could turn a potato into a puppy. That's when I figured out what had happened."

"Are you mad?" I asked. "I know it was wrong to trick you. I didn't realize it until later, and then it was too late."

"If I hadn't been so hard-nosed and stubborn, you wouldn't have had to use tricks. When I saw the look on Lost Deer's face when he hugged his puppy, I knew I'd been wrong. If I'd been more open and willing to listen to you, and not so sure I was always right and everyone else was always wrong, we could have

233

worked it out." He laughed again. "I'll forgive you, if you'll forgive me."

I smiled as I felt that small bit of guilt slip out of my heart. "A watermelon change into a pony?" I asked, and we all laughed together.

LOST DEER

I think that there are two of me,
Myself and another,
Be he looks exactly like me,
So it can't be my brother.

Sometimes when I wake up,
I feel like being bad;
I stomp and throw my toys,
And get so doggone mad!

I am a terrible grouch,
Then nothing goes right;
I want to jump right back in bed
And pretend that it's still night.

My shoes are on the wrong feet,
My shirt is backward side out,
I throw myself on the floor
And kick and scream and pout.

I wish I was a grown-up man
And very, very old—
I would never wear any clothes,
Except when it was cold.

I get so mad I want to cry,
And then I want to shout,
But then my mom would want to know,
"What's it all about?"

I sit on my bed with my chin in my hand,
And wish that I was a grown-up man,
And then my Mom tiptoes in
And looks at me with a cheerful grin.

She asks if she can help me dress,
But I can dress myself, I guess!
I grin at her, and I'm so glad,
That she doesn't know that I was mad.

I grab my pants and I
Pull on my clothes,
And my T-shirt doesn't even
Catch on my nose.

Mom hugs me and fixes my breakfast,
And I'm as cheerful as I can be,
Because I don't want her to know
About the "other" me!

Chapter Twenty-Nine

The summer sun was setting red and wild behind the mountains as Don and I stood hand in hand on the rocky hill overlooking our home.

The children were busy running between the tall pines and hiding from each other.

Little Antelope had grown tall. He was quiet and thoughtful and sensitive, and I knew our firstborn would always make us proud.

Lost Deer was all laughter and jokes, and he teased his little brother until he was in tears. Lost Deer could always make anyone laugh, even on his worst days. Life would be easier for him than for most.

Snow Cloud was small for his age and sometimes difficult to understand, but he had the face of an angel and would grow up to do great things.

And Spring Storm, our chubby bundle of love! How precious you are, my daughter; what joy you bring!

Spring Storm toddled over to me and handed me a dandelion she had crushed in her chubby hand.

I took it and held it to my lips and kissed it. Sunshine flowers! What memories you hold!

I looked at Don, my wonderful, strong, patient husband. My anchor, my rock, my great love.

He turned and caught me watching him and smiled.

"I think next spring we can get you a horse," he said.

"A horse! I'll have a horse!" I was thrilled. "With a horse I will be an Indian again!"

"Crying Wind, you have never stopped being an Indian! You will always belong in the sunset past of a hundred years ago. The rest of the world is living in the twentieth century and talking of rockets to Mars. You live in the eighteenth century and talk of horses running across the open desert. You have always been an Indian; you always will be. Your wildness was born into our children. I can see it in their eyes. The mountains, the wind, call to them and make them restless. Look at them now, running through the trees—they aren't just children playing, they are more like wild horses thundering through the valley." My husband said sadly, "They are your children, Crying Wind. How little of my blood they have."

"But they look like you." I wanted to take the sadness out of his voice.

"Yes, their skin is fair and their hair is yellow, but in their black eyes is the look of wildness I once saw on the face of a Kickapoo maid in a forest long ago." He smiled.

For so long life had seemed like a handful of dust, but when I had surrendered my life to God, He had filled my emptiness, taken away my fear, and put peace into my heart.

"I have everything, everything in the world!" I smiled.

Don's hand folded around mine and we began to walk toward the cabin.

Our three strong sons ran far ahead of us, laughing and shouting for us to hurry. Spring Storm toddled at our side.

The sun was going down, and the sky and earth looked golden.

Crying Wind had come home at last. *The End*

CHRISTIAN HERALD ASSOCIATION AND ITS MINISTRIES

CHRISTIAN HERALD ASSOCIATION, founded in 1878, publishes The Christian Herald Magazine, one of the leading interdenominational religious monthlies in America. Through its wide circulation, it brings inspiring articles and the latest news of religious developments to many families. From the magazine's pages came the initiative for CHRISTIAN HERALD CHILDREN'S HOME and THE BOWERY MISSION, two individually supported not-for-profit corporations.

CHRISTIAN HERALD CHILDREN'S HOME, established in 1894, is the name for a unique and dynamic ministry to disadvantaged children, offering hope and opportunities which would not otherwise be available for reasons of poverty and neglect. The goal is to develop each child's potential and to demonstrate Christian compassion and understanding to children in need.

Mont Lawn is a permanent camp located in Bushkill, Pennsylvania. It is the focal point of a ministry which provides a healthful "vacation with a purpose" to children who without it would be confined to the streets of the city. Up to 1000 children between the ages of 7 and 11 come to Mont Lawn each year.

Christian Herald Children's Home maintains year-round contact with children by means of an *In-City Youth Ministry*. Central to its philosophy is the belief that only through sustained relationships and demonstrated concern can individual lives be truly enriched. Special emphasis is on individual guidance, spiritual and family counseling and tutoring. This follow-up ministry to inner-city children culminates for many in financial assistance toward higher education and career counseling.

THE BOWERY MISSION, located at 227 Bowery, New York City, has since 1879 been reaching out to the lost men on the Bowery, offering them what could be their last chance to rebuild their lives. Every man is fed, clothed and ministered to. Countless numbers have entered the 90-day residential rehabilitation program at the Bowery Mission. A concentrated ministry of counseling, medical care, nutrition therapy, Bible study and Gospel services awakens a man to spiritual renewal within himself.

These ministries are supported solely by the voluntary contributions of individuals and by legacies and bequests. Contributions are tax deductible. Checks should be made out either to CHRISTIAN HERALD CHILDREN'S HOME or to THE BOWERY MISSION.

Administrative Office: 40 Overlook Drive, Chappaqua, New York 10514
Telephone: (914) 769-9000